Football HANDBOOK 2004-2005

Lisa Regan

Matt Parselle

BARDFIELD
PRESS

PERSONAL INFORMATION

Full Name ....

Date of Birth ....

Address ....

....

....

....

....

Phone ....

E-mail ....

....

Height ....

Weight ....

FAVOURITE THINGS

Singer ....

Band ....

Actor/Actress ....

....

Film ....

....

TV programme ....

....

Sport ....

Team ....

Hobby ....

Book ....

School subject ....

Use this page to keep a record of any important dates, as well as all the birthdays of your family and friends.

IMPORTANT DATES

2004

August
30............Summer Bank Holiday

September
16............Jewish New Year

October
31............Hallowe'en

November
5..............Bonfire Night
11............Remembrance Day
30............St Andrew's Day

December
21............Winter Solstice
25............Christmas Day
26............Boxing Day

2005

January
1..............New Years Day

February
9..............Chinese New Year
14............St Valentine's Day

March
1..............St David's Day
17............St Patrick's Day
25............Good Friday
26............Easter Sunday
28............Easter Monday

April
23............St George's Day

May
2..............May Day Bank Holiday
30............Spring Bank Holiday

June
21............Summer Solstice

July
4..............Independence Day (USA)
14............Bastille Day (France)

BIRTHDAYS

January

February

March

April

May

June

July

August

September

October

November

December

Play the Game

Are you totally football crazy? Do you play football, watch football, dream football, eat and drink football?! Then read on for lots of vital info on your favourite sport.

Ye olden days

Football has been played, in various forms, for hundreds of years. Early versions were played in Ancient Greece, China and Rome – imagine saving your pocket money for the latest 'team toga' in home and away colours!

In England, footie was played by huge teams of villagers, who would basically kick anything kind of ball-shaped around the village. It's said that a popular ball was made of a stuffed animal bladder – yuk! Wonder what they used for goal posts – piles of bones?!

At one time, football was banned by the king of England because people were playing footie instead of practising useful battle sports like archery!

By 1843, the game was popular all around the country, but everyone used different rules. Before teams could play proper matches against each other, they had to write down standard rules. Soon, competitions were played all over the land, and by 1872 the FA Cup tournament had been organized. By 1901 over 100,000 fans gathered to watch the FA Cup final!

Name of the game

Your fave game is called many things. Some people call it 'soccer', especially in the US where football is completely different (you've seen the huge, padded-up players running around the gridiron carrying the ball). Soccer is short for 'Association Football',

footie's full name. That helps rugby fans tell the difference, as they call their game Rugby Football. Nothing's ever easy! However, we know what we're talking about, and football is football in this book. Football is now hugely popular all around the world. The World Cup was first played in 1930, and nowadays is the world's most popular sporting competition, with the finals being watched by a total of over 30 billion people!

Footie fact

In most European countries, football is called something which sounds similar to the English, or is a translation of the words 'foot' and 'ball'. For example, in French you'll hear 'le football' and in German it's 'fussball'. However, in Italy you'd never guess what they're talking about – it's called 'calcio', after their own historical version of the game.

Who's in charge?

As football became more popular, and rules were standardized, different sets of people called 'governing bodies' were set up around the world to watch over the way the game is run. FIFA organizes football at a global (world) level. The initials stand for Fédération Internationale de Football Association (International Federation of Association Football). FIFA organizes the World Cup competitions.

During the World Cup, you may hear talk of other organizations such as UEFA and CONCACAF. These are smaller groups that oversee football in each continent. CONCACAF is the group for North and Central America and the Caribbean. Asia, Africa, South America, Oceania and Europe each have their own regional body looking after them.

In Europe, it's UEFA and it organizes the European club competitions(such as the European Championships), and the club competitions (such as the Champions League and, funnily enough!, the UEFA Cup). At a lower level again, the FA is the Football Association of England, which is the oldest of all the national associations in the world.

If you're keen to play football at the highest level, here are some heroes to show you what's possible for a football genius!

Famous Players

Pelé

This Brazilian footballer is a legend – all football fans have heard how great he was, even if they never saw him play. His full name is Edson Arantes do Nascimento and he played in the 1950s, 60s and 70s. He was nicknamed The Black Pearl.

Pelé first played (and scored) for Brazil in 1957 when he was only 16, and went on to earn 93 caps and score an average of one goal every game. He also won three World Cup winners' medals, the first at the age of 17 when he scored twice in the final.

At club level, Pelé played for Santos FC and had an amazing career. He averaged over 100 goals a season several times, and his best record was 139 goals in 1958. He holds the world record for most hat tricks (92) and most international goals (97). Altogether, his career lasted over 20 years, and he scored 1280 goals in 1360 games. Unbelievable!

Zinedine Zidane

Still the world's most expensive player (he cost £48 million when Real Madrid bought him from Juventus in 2001) many people think his fee was totally justified as he's the best player in the world. Zidane was named FIFA World Player of the Year in 1998, 2000 and 2003. He has led the French national team to victory in the World Cup – scoring twice himself against the mighty Brazil – and followed that with victory in the European Championships.

Just Fontaine

This French player is not as well known as Pelé, but still holds the record he set in the 1958 World Cup finals, where he scored an amazing 13 goals. Fontaine's career ended early through injury, but he still managed to play 20 internationals and score 27 goals.

Alfredo di Stefano

An Argentinian playing in Spain in the 1950s and 60s, di Stefano is remembered as an important part of Real Madrid's success in the European Cup. The competition started in 1956 and they won it the first five times in a row, with di Stefano scoring each time. He was a great goalscorer, with seven goals in seven international games, eight times top scorer in his league, and a total of 554 goals in 698 matches.

The Blond Arrow

Di Stefano had the nickname The Blond Arrow because of his speed on the pitch, and was arguably the best club player in Europe at that time, although injury prevented him making his name in the World Cup.

David Beckham

All football fans have heard of Beckham, and all England fans remember the bad days before today's times of hero worship. A great all-round player, Beckham has gone from the country's most hated man, being sent off in the 1998 World Cup, to its most famous (and most expensive) football export. He cost Real Madrid £25 million when they bought him from Manchester United in 2003, but is worth a fortune in advertising fees and merchandizing deals.

He scored his first goal for Man United in 1995, and his credits include six Premiership titles, two FA Cup winners' medals, UEFA Champions League winners, captain of club and country, BBC Sports Personality of the Year, runner-up in World Player of the Year awards (twice) and an OBE from the Queen!

CUP WINNERS

Despite what people say, football's not just about taking part – it's about winning. All clubs and international sides are proud of the cups they've won. Take a look through these trophy cabinets!

World Cup

Uruguay won the first ever World Cup, played in 1930. However, Brazil have the most impressive World Cup record. They've won the most times (five) and are the only team to have won it away from their own continent (winning it in North America and Asia as well as South America). In 1970 they were allowed to keep the original trophy (called the Jules Rimet Trophy after the man who 'invented' the World Cup) for winning it three times!

Although England is the home of football, its national team have only won the World Cup once. (That was in 1966, but shame on you if you call yourself a footie fan and didn't know that!) The final was played at Wembley, between England and West Germany, and the score was 2–2 after 90 minutes. The game went to extra time, and the final result was England 4 West Germany 2. Phew! England's Geoff Hurst became the first (and only) man to score a hat-trick in a World Cup final, and Martin Peters scored the other goal.

FA Cup

This is the world's oldest cup competition, started way back in 1872 when it was won by a team called Wanderers. WHO?! In fact, several of the early winners are teams who don't exist any more, such as Clapham Rovers, Old Carthusians and Royal Engineers. Back then, the final was played at different venues, too; it wasn't until 1923 that it settled at Wembley, where it was staged for nearly 80 years.

You can see how unpredictable the competition is by looking at the number of teams who've won over the years. If you turn to the back of this book, you'll see the Top Ten teams who've won the most times. But what you don't see is that a total of 42 different teams have won the cup, including clubs such as Huddersfield Town, Blackpool, Cardiff and Preston North End, who aren't such big names nowadays!

Champions League

This used to be called the European Cup, but was renamed in 1999. It is competed for by clubs finishing at or near the top of the leagues of all the main European nations. Thirty-two sides start off in groups, and the 16 teams who qualify carry on as far as possible through a knockout competition.

The competition started in 1955, and initially the Cup was won an amazing five times in a row by Real Madrid! It wasn't until the late 1960s that British clubs started to make their mark, with Celtic and Man United holding up the Cup. Since then, Liverpool have shown good form with four wins, and Notts Forest and Aston Villa have also won the competition.

Man United are particularly proud of their victory in 1999, when the Cup was part of their treble-winning season (they also won the English League and FA Cup): they beat Bayern Munich 2–1, although non-United fans would argue that they were extremely lucky. They trailed 0–1 until Teddy Sheringham set up the winning goal for Solskjaer a minute later, avoiding extra time!

UEFA Cup

This is entered by cup winners and other main sides from European nations. Crowd trouble and football hooliganism led to English sides being banned from European competitions during the late 1980s. Despite that, English teams have won the UEFA Cup ten times, more than any other country except Italy, although Spanish teams won five of the first six trophies.

Liverpool have a great record in the UEFA Cup competition. In 1973 they became the first side to do the double of winning the UEFA Cup and League, and then did it again in 1976. In 2001 they became the first side ever to win the UEFA Cup, FA Cup and League Cup all together. Wow!

Manchester United players celebrate winning three cups in 1999

In the Club

You probably know the big clubs of today's Premiership, but who are the clubs to watch in other countries? Don't forget, football would be very boring if everyone supported the same top teams, so follow your chosen club with pride, even if they're not so rich and famous!

British names to know

So many clubs, so many cups, championships and histories. Let's start with Scotland...

Rangers and **Celtic** dominate the Scottish Premier League. Between them, the two Glasgow clubs have won the title every year since 1986, and many times before then!

Further south, **Man United** are certainly the richest and probably the most famous English club, and some think the best. They have won the English Premiership eight times since it began in 1992/93, and are the only club to have won the treble (in 1999, when they won the League, the FA Cup and the European Cup).

Let's not forget **Arsenal**, who've spent longer in the first/Premier division without relegation than any other club, and were the first to win the FA and League Cups in the same season. They've won the FA Cup/Championship double three times. They must also be the only team to have a manager (Arsene Wenger) whose name is nearly the same as the club!

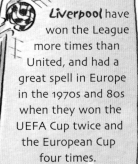

Liverpool have won the League more times than United, and had a great spell in Europe in the 1970s and 80s when they won the UEFA Cup twice and the European Cup four times.

South American giant

European fans are able to watch South America's greatest players every week in the Spanish, Italian and English leagues. Players like Ronaldo, Crespo and Kleberson are heroes in Europe as well as their home continent. It wasn't always that way. One big reason that people loved to watch the Brazilian team in the World Cup was that they didn't often see them play, and their skills were just unbelievable.

European dream teams

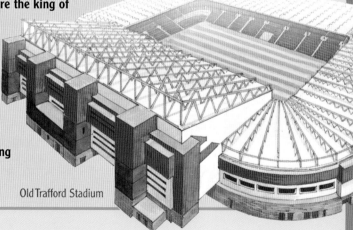

Every country in Europe plays football, but some countries are more famous for their soccer talents than others. Many British fans tune in to watch matches in the Serie A (Italian league), Bundesliga (Germany) and La Liga (Spain).

Here are some teams you should know:

AC Milan and **Inter Milan**: Both teams from the Italian city are world-class with amazing players. AC Milan play in red and black stripes, Inter wear blue and black stripes.

Juventus: Winners of the European Cup and UEFA Cup, many star footballers have played for this team who are based in Turin. (Watch out for another Italian side whose name hides their home town, too: Lazio play in Rome.)

Bayern Munich: One of the greatest German clubs, they have won just about every title going since they formed in 1900. In the 1970s their main rivals were Borussia Moenchengladbach, but that's way too hard to spell to be able to be a fan!

Real Madrid: Many Spanish teams have 'Real' in their name – it means royal. Madrid are the king of clubs, though, named FIFA's 'Team of the Century' in 1998. Beat that!

Olympique Marseille: Marseille are one of France's best sides, but are also infamous for winning the European Cup in 1993 then having it taken away as punishment for match-fixing.

Old Trafford Stadium

The world's greatest players like Pelé never played European club football. Instead, teams like Santos, Cruzeiro and Palmeiros (Brazil), River Plate, Boca Juniors and Independiente (Argentina) and Peñarol (Uruguay) were flamboyant, skilful sides. They still all compete against each other for the Copa Libertadores, which has been won the most times (seven) by Independiente.

Rules and Regulations

Watching and playing football is great entertainment, but it helps if you understand what's going on. If you play, it's good to know for sure what the rules are. The official FIFA rule book is about 70 pages long, so here are some simple but vital highlights.

Red and Yellow cards

If you're shown a red card by the referee, that's it – you've been sent off. If it's only a yellow, you're on a warning – another yellow in the same game and you'll be sent off, too. Both times, your name will be written in the ref's book – 'Uh-oh, you've been booked!' At the same time, a free kick may be awarded.

Red cards are obviously given for more serious offences, such as serious fouls. Watch out, because you might not think the offence deserves a sending off. They include spitting at another player, using offensive language and deliberately touching the ball with your hand or lower arm (handball) to prevent a goal going in the net.

Offside!

Everyone jokes about people who don't understand the offside rule, but it's not that tricky. Basically, if you're closer to the opposing goal line (the one you want to score in) than a forward played ball and your second last opponent (including the goalkeeper), you're in an offside position. The ref can then give an indirect free kick to the other team. However, the ref won't give a free kick if you're offside direct from a throw in, corner or goal-kick (taken by the opposing team), or are in your own half. The ref can also let play continue if you're not directly interfering with play, or gaining an advantage, by being offside. Be careful, though – you can be offside if the ball is kicked to someone else on your team and you're in the wrong position. That will make your team EXTREMELY cross!

Extra time

In a normal league match, it doesn't matter if the end result is a draw — both sides get equal points. In a knockout game, though, one team has to win to go through. For certain competitions, extra time is added on to the end of the 90-minute match to try to end up with a winner.

Originally, extra time was a definite extra 30 minutes added on (15 minutes in each direction). In Euro 96, the Golden Goal rule was first used. Here, a goal by either team stopped play instantly — the goalscorers were the winners outright.

However, this has recently been adapted to the Silver Goal rule. To stop teams playing too defensively in a Golden Goal situation, the first 15 minutes are played to see if either team takes the lead. If the score is still equal, the last 15 minutes in the opposite direction are played.

Remember: extra time is not the same as 'stoppage time', which is time (usually a couple of minutes) added on by the ref to make up for time lost during injuries, substitutions, lst balls and so on.

Free kicks

Free kicks are great. The opposing team line up in a wall and look a bit daft, someone cool like Beckham kicks the ball and bends it around the defence into goal, HURRAY! Right?

Wrong. That's only possible if it's a direct free kick. The first touch of the ball is allowed to send the ball directly into goal, unless an opposing player can legally stop it. If this kind of free kick is given for a foul in the penalty area, it's a penalty kick.

Sometimes, free kicks are indirect. These are given for less serious offences, such as obstructing an opponent. In these cases, a goal only counts if the ball has touched a second player after the free kick is taken.

Silky Skills

So much for being a football fan and knowing all there is to know about the famous names and the rules of watching from your living room. It's time to put yourself to the test and see if you can play! Here are some superb ball skills that everyone would love to master. Remember, they can sound easier than they are, so practice is the only way to become skilful!

Curling the ball

Can you 'bend it like Beckham'? You can if you hit the ball correctly, with the proper part of your foot. You need to strike the ball off-centre, so use the very outside or the very inside of your boot. As your foot makes contact with the ball, twist it slightly — this is known as 'wrapping your foot around the ball' and is part of Beckham's killer kick. Make sure you follow through properly after the ball has left your foot.

Volleying

It's harder to kick the ball when it's in the air than when it's sitting still on the ground. It's even harder to kick it (accurately, anyway) before it has bounces. That's volleying the ball — and that's why you need to practise.

Usually, if you want to pass the ball to a team-mate, you will control it first. If you're faced with an open goal and a floundering keeper, you might not have time to control the ball. You simply want to boot it into goal!

Timing the kick right, and keeping your eye on the ball, are both vital. Watch the ball constantly as you raise your kicking foot, making sure you stay balanced on the other foot. Keep your head over the ball (so you're not leaning backwards) to stop the ball flying high over the crossbar. Make contact with the side of your foot or your instep, if possible. Hitting the ball with the top of your foot is more likely to send it flying in the wrong direction. Aim at goal, and don't forget to follow through (even if it results in you landing on the floor!).

Overhead kicks

There are several things to remember before you attempt this spectacular kick. First, the reason it's so cool is because it's so difficult. Even Pelé said that he scored a tiny number of his 1,000 goals in this way. Second, if it goes wrong, you'll feel silly, and your team-mates may be cross that you didn't just pass to someone else instead of showing off.

So you've got to be sure you can do it!

Third, if you do it wrong, you could really hurt yourself. Practise kicking and landing, using your arms and non-kicking foot to break the fall. Use a soft ball and make sure there's nothing to break within a few kilometres all round!

When you're ready, here goes. Take off with your kicking leg and lean back with your other leg raised. Keep your eye on the ball, and bring your kicking leg over to hit the ball with your instep. Your leg should be stretched, toes forward, to get over the ball. Your other leg will drop to balance you (which is why this kick is sometimes called a scissor kick). Land carefully as you've practised, making sure your back, neck or shoulders don't break your fall.

August 2004

	school notes/homework	what's on this week
monday **2**		
tuesday **3**		
wednesday **4**		
thursday **5**	Wayne Bridge, 24 today	
friday **6**		
saturday **7**	Nationwide League starts today	
sunday **8**	Community Shield held in Cardiff Louis Saha, 26 today	

FACTS OF THE WEEK

LUCKY CHARMS

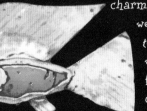

Egyptians wore lucky charms called amulets. The charms were meant to protect the wearer from evil spirits and to bring good luck. Children wore amulets shaped like fish to protect them from drowning in the river Nile.

A DAY CAN LAST 21 HOURS!

Night and day happen because Earth is spinning as it circles the Sun. At the height of summer, places near the North Pole are so tilted towards the Sun that it is light almost all day long.

CANTERBURY TALES

In the 1300s an Englishman called Geoffrey Chaucer wrote 'The Canterbury Tales.' These stories were about a group of pilgrims travelling from a London inn to a religious site in Canterbury.

JOKE OF THE WEEK

"Why couldn't the team have anything to drink?"
"Because they'd lost all the cups"

QUICK QUIZ

1. Which country does Ronaldo play for?
2. Which team did Holland beat 5–0 during the 1998 World Cup?
3. Who used to play their home games at Roker Park?
4. Who are known as the Magpies?
5. Which nation has Don Hutchinson played for?
6. Who replaced George Graham as manager of Spurs in 2001?

1. Brazil 2. South Korea 3. Sunderland 4. Newcastle United 5. Scotland 6. Glenn Hoddle

ODD ONE OUT

Which of these four countries is the ODD ONE OUT and why?

SPAIN, INDIA, GERMANY, GREECE

India – All the others are European countries

August 2004

	school notes/homework	what's on this week
monday **9**		
tuesday **10**	Roy Keane, 33 today	
wednesday **11**		
thursday **12**		
friday **13**	Alan Shearer, 34 today	
saturday **14**	Premiership season starts today Jay-Jay Okocha, 31 today	
sunday **15**		

FACTS OF THE WEEK

THE WEATHER FOR LAST WEEK

The earliest weather records are over 3000 years old. They were found on a piece of tortoiseshell and had been written down by Chinese weather watchers. The inscriptions describe when it rained or snowed and how windy it was.

WHEN THE UNITED STATES DOUBLED UP

Louisiana Purchase

In 1803 the American president, Thomas Jefferson, bought a massive area of land called Louisiana from the French. This was known as the Louisiana Purchase, and included all the land between the Mississippi and the Rocky Mountains.

A STRANGE SIGHT

The Matamata turtle lives only in South America. It is one of the strangest of all turtles, as its head is almost flat, and is shaped like a triangle. It lies on the bottom of rivers and eats fish that swim past.

JOKE OF THE WEEK

"What do a footballer and a magician have in common?"
"They both like hat tricks"

ODD ONE OUT

Which one of these four is the ODD ONE OUT and why?

BOXER, PERSIAN, SPANIEL, TERRIER

PERSIAN – All the others are breeds of dog

August 2004

	school notes/homework	what's on this week
monday **16**		
tuesday **17**	Thierry Henry, 27 today	
wednesday **18**		
thursday **19**		
friday **20**		
saturday **21**		
sunday **22**		

FACTS OF THE WEEK

RECORD BREAKERS!

A single boat towed 100 waterskiers! This record was achieved off the coast of Australia in 1986 and no one has beaten it yet. The drag boat was a cruiser called Reef Cat.

KEEP OUT OF ITS WAY!

A tornado is the fastest wind on Earth – it can spin at speeds of 500 kilometres an hour. Tornadoes form over ground that has become very warm. This fast-rising funnel acts as a vacuum cleaner, destroying buildings and lifting cars into the air.

MILLIONS OF YEARS AGO

Dinosaurs lived between 230 million and 65 million years ago. This vast length of time is called the Mesozoic Era. Dinosaurs were around for about 80 times longer than people have been on Earth!

JOKE OF THE WEEK

Ref: "I'm sending you off"   Player: "What for?"
Ref: "The rest of the match!"

QUICK QUIZ

1. Which country has Ramon Vega represented?
2. Upton Park is the homeground for which club?
3. Which veteran defender broke his leg twice in 1999–2000?
4. What nationality is striker Sergei Rebrov?
5. At which club did Dennis Bergkamp begin his career?
6. With which club was Bobby Moore when he was made captain of England?

1. Switzerland 2. West Ham 3. Stuart Pearce 4. Ukrainian 5. Ajax 6. West Ham

WORD SEARCH

Try and find five English counties hidden in the word search below:

```
N Q N I F S D S
O K E N T A L U
R W D W O P S S
F S E S S E X S
O C W I P K D E
L I P D S G M X
K S U R R E Y T
M U M F O R A B
```

August 2004

	school notes/homework	what's on this week
monday **23** Glen Johnson, 20 today		
tuesday **24** Tugay Kerimoglu, 34 today		
wednesday **25**		
thursday **26**		
friday **27** European Super Cup held in Monaco Dietmar Hamann, 31 today		
saturday **28**		
sunday **29** Celestine Babayaro, 26 today		

FACTS OF THE WEEK

KEEP AN EYE OUT

A meteor shower is a dramatic display of shooting stars. For a short period more than a thousand a second may flash across the sky. August is the best month to see one.

NEW SHOES

Booby birds dance to attract a mate. There are two types of booby, blue-or red-footed. The dancing draws attention to the male's colourful feet. Perhaps this stops the females from mating with the wrong type of bird.

WHAT A DOG!

A dog named Laika was the first living thing to go into space. In 1957 she travelled in a Russian spacecraft called 'Sputnik 2', and stayed in space for two weeks.

JOKE OF THE WEEK

"Why do artists never win when they play football?"
"Because they keep drawing!"

QUICK QUIZ

1. What country have both Bebeto and Roberto Carlos played for?
2. Which club's ground is known as Stamford Bridge?
3. Elland Road is the home of which Yorkshire side?
4. What surname links England players Ashley, Andy and Joe?
5. Glenn Hoddle and Gianluca Vialli have both managed which club?
6. Who scored the winning goal in England's 2000 clash with Germany?

1. Brazil 2. Chelsea f 3. Leeds 4. Cole 5. Tottenham Hotspur 6. Alan Shearer

ODD ONE OUT

Can you spot the odd band out?

BUSTED, WESTLIFE, ATOMIC KITTEN, BLUE

Atomic Kitten – All the others are boys only

	school notes/homework	what's on this week
monday **30**		
tuesday **31**		
wednesday **1**		
thursday **2** Freddie Kanoute, 27 today		
friday **3** Gerard Houllier, 57 today		
saturday **4**		**2006 FIFA World Cup™** England v Austria Wales v Azerbaijan Northern Ireland v Poland Republic of Ireland v Cyprus
sunday **5**		

FACTS OF THE WEEK

MAKING MUSIC

Most crickets chirp by rubbing together their wings. The bases of the wings near the body have hard, ridged strips like rows of pegs. These click past each other to make the chirping sound.

UNDERSEA GOD

Neptune (or Poseidon) was an undersea god. Poseidon was the name used by the ancient Greeks and Neptune by the ancient Romans. Both civilizations pictured their god with a fork called a trident. They blamed their gods for the terrible storms that wrecked boats in the Mediterranean.

EUREKA!

A scientist called Archimedes lived in Greece over 2000 years ago. He made some important discoveries in physics and mathematics. He made one discovery while in the bath and ran into the street without any clothes, shouting "Eureka!" which means 'I have found it'.

JOKE OF THE WEEK

"Which part of a football pitch smells the nicest?"
"The scenter spot!"

NAME SCRAMBLE

A former member of a girl band and wife to a famous footballer, is hidden in these letters. Who is it?

ITVCIOAR CHMAKBE

VICTORIA BECKHAM

September 2004

	school notes/homework	what's on this week
monday **6**	Carlo Cudicini, 31 today	
tuesday **7**	Stephane Henchoz, 30 today	
wednesday **8**		**2006 FIFA World Cup™** England v Poland Wales v Northern Ireland Scotland v Slovenia Republic of Ireland v Switzerland
thursday **9**		
friday **10**		
saturday **11**		
sunday **12**	David Thompson, 27 today	

FACTS OF THE WEEK

FLOWING SEAS

There are streams in the oceans. All the water in the oceans is constantly moving, but in some places it flows as currents, which take particular paths. One of these is the warm Gulf Stream, that travels around the edge of the Atlantic Ocean.

LOVING TO DEATH!

Courtship is a dangerous time for the hunting insect called the praying mantis. The female is much bigger than the male, and as soon as they have mated, she may eat him!

RECORD BREAKING ROBOT

Jurassic Park's nine species of dinosaurs thundered and roared through the world's cinemas in 1993. Made of latex and foam rubber, the dinosaur robots were incredibly realistic. They included the largest film robot ever made a – 5.5-m tall Tyrannosaurus rex.

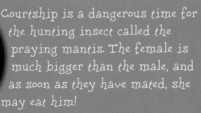

JOKE OF THE WEEK

"Why aren't football stadiums built in outer space?"
"Because there's just no atmosphere!"

WORD SEARCH

Find the five BIRDS OF PREY hiding in this word search

```
E A G L E E W Q
V U L T U R E W
U B U Z Z A R D
L E A R O D O E
T F A L C O N P
N B S O W L C D
P M C E W T Y U
A J K I S F A B
```

September 2004

	school notes/homework	what's on this week
monday **13**		
tuesday **14**		
wednesday **15**	Eidur Gudjohnsen, 26 today	
thursday **16**		
friday **17**	Marcel Desailly, 36 today	
saturday **18**	Sol Campbell, 30 today	
sunday **19**		

FACTS OF THE WEEK

WATERSPORT

Jetskiers can travel at nearly 100 kilometres per hour. Jetskis were developed in the 1960s. Their inventor was an American called Clayton Jacobsen who wanted to combine his two favourite hobbies – motorbikes and waterskiing.

WELL TRAINED

It took about 14 years of training to become a knight. The son of a noble joined a lord's household aged seven. After training he became a squire, and he learned how to fight with a sword. If successful, he became a knight at 21.

FIGHTING FOR HUMAN RIGHTS

Nelson Mandela was the first black president of South Africa (1994-99). As a young man he fought for the rights of black South Africans. White leaders imprisoned him for his beliefs for 28 years (1962-90).

JOKE OF THE WEEK

"What's the chilliest ground in the Premiership?"
"Cold Trafford!"

QUICK QUIZ

1. Which club's ground is known as The Valley?
2. With which club did John Barnes begin his career?
3. Which team plays their home games at Ibrox?
4. Where were the 1994 World Cup finals staged?
5. What colours do Celtic play in?
6. Who did Chelsea defeat in the 2000 FA Cup final?

1. Charlton Athletic 2. Watford 3. Rangers 4. USA 5. Green and white 6. Aston Villa

WORD SCRAMBLE

Unscramble the letters to find three famous cities:

DADIRM, HTANES, EOMR

MADRID, ATHENS, ROME

September 2004

	school notes/homework	what's on this week
monday **20**	Henrik Larsson, 33 today	
tuesday **21**		
wednesday **22**	Ronaldo, 28 today Harry Kewell, 26 today	
thursday **23**		
friday **24**	John Arne Riise, 24 today	
saturday **25**		
sunday **26**	Michael Ballack, 28 today	

FACTS OF THE WEEK

LOVE DANCE

Some insects flash bright lights as they fly. The firefly is not a fly but a type of beetle. In a courtship display the male fireflies 'dance' in the air at dusk, the rear parts of their bodies glowing on and off about once each second.

SINKING SUCCESS

'Titanic' (US 1997) is the only film since 'Ben-Hur' (US 1959) to have won 11 oscars. More than 100 stunt artists helped to recreate the sinking scene. The stunt team spent a record 6000 hours on the set of 'Titanic' – the equivalent of almost 17 years for one person!

WHAT'S IN A NAME?

The most common family name in the world is probably Zhiang – 1 in 10 Chinese are called Zhiang. In the Islamic world it is Muhammad, and in the English-speaking world it is Smith. The shortest name is O, common among Koreans.

NAME SCRAMBLE

Which famous footballer is hidden in these letters?

DONALRO

RONALDO

JOKE OF THE WEEK

"How did the football pitch end up as a triangle?"
"Somebody took a corner!"

	school notes/homework	what's on this week
monday **27**	Francis Totti, 28 today	
tuesday **28**		
wednesday **29**		
thursday **30**		
friday **1**	Pelé plays his last match and retires from football, 1977	
saturday **2**		
sunday **3**	Anthony Le Tallec, 20 today	

FACTS OF THE WEEK

CAMELOT

King Arthur had many castle homes but his favourite was Camelot. Historians think that Camelot was really an English castle called Tintagel. The remains of this castle can still be explored in the county of Cornwall.

SOME WERE REALLY CUTE!

The name 'dinosaur' means 'terrible lizard'. But dinosaurs weren't lizards, and not all dinosaurs were terrible. Small plant-eating dinosaurs were about as 'terrible' as today's sheep!

WHAT LIES BENEATH

Long ago, people believed in a giant sea monster, called the kraken. The stories were used to explain the dangers of the sea. Sightings of the giant squid with eyes as big as dinner plates, might have inspired these tales.

LETTER PUZZLE

Where would you see these letters shown in this order?

ZXCVBNM

On a typewriter or computer keyboard

JOKE OF THE WEEK

"Which goalkeeper can jump higher than a crossbar?"
"All of them, a crossbar can't jump!"

October 2004

	school notes/homework	what's on this week
monday **4**		
tuesday **5**		
wednesday **6**		
thursday **7**	England play their last game at Wembley (*losing 1–0 to Germany*), 2000	
friday **8**		
saturday **9**		**2006 FIFA World Cup™** England v Wales Northern Ireland v Azerbaijan Scotland v Norway Republic of Ireland v France
sunday **10**	Dean Kiely, 34 today	

FACTS OF THE WEEK

CHANGE OF HORSE

A rich medieval knight would have three horses. He rode his heaviest horse for fighting and tournaments. He also had a horse for riding, and a baggage horse. The best horses were warhorses from Italy and Spain. They were quick, strong and sturdy.

TRICK OF THE LIGHT

Oceans can look blue, green or grey. This is because of the way light hits the surface. Water soaks up the red parts of light but scatters the blue-green parts, making the sea look different shades of blue or green.

STICKY FEET

The gecko is a lizard found in most warm countries. The tree gecko has hairs on its feet, which have a sticking effect. This enables it to walk on any surface, and even hang on by just one toe!

JOKE OF THE WEEK

"Why are football players never asked out for dinner?"
"Because they're always dribbling!"

QUICK QUIZ

1. Who captained England in their World Cup-winning campaign?
2. Which club's nickname is the Gunners?
3. Which country won the 1994 World Cup?
4. Who won Euro 2000?
5. Which club play their home games at the Reebok Stadium?
6. Leeds paid West Ham £18 million for which defender during the 2000–01 season?

1. Bobby Moore 2. Arsenal 3. Brazil 4. France 5. Bolton Wanderers 6. Rio Ferdinand

ODD ONE OUT

Which of these four is the ODD ONE OUT and why?

REMBRANT, CONSTABLE, MONET, SHAKESPEARE

SHAKESPEARE – All the others are artists

	school notes/homework	what's on this week
monday **11**		
tuesday **12**	Shola Ameobi, 23 today	
wednesday **13**	Wes Brown, 25 today Scott Parker, 24 today	**2006 FIFA World Cup™** England v Azerbaijan Wales v Poland Northern Ireland v Austria Scotland v Moldova Republic of Ireland v Faroe Islands
thursday **14**		
friday **15**	Paul Robinson, 25 today	
saturday **16**		
sunday **17**		

FACTS OF THE WEEK

AM I AN INSECT?

A spider has eight legs.
So it's not an insect!
It's a type of animal
called an
arachnid. All spiders
are deadly hunters. They have large
fanglike jaws which they use to grab and
stab their prey. The fangs inject a poison to kill
or quieten the victim before being eaten.

WORST EVER HURRICANE IN BRITAIN

Britain's worst storm of modern
times was the hurricane of
October, 1987. High winds uprooted
and blew down 15 million trees
in southern England, blocked
roads, and brought down roofs
and power lines.

DANGEROUS WORK

Marie Curie and her husband Pierre were
scientists who worked in France in
the late 1800s and early 1900s. Marie
Curie was a clever and hard-
working physicist who discovered a
dangerous but useful chemical
substance called radium.

JOKE OF THE WEEK

"What lights up a football stadium?"
"A football match!"

BIRD SEARCH

Try and find the five garden birds hidden in the word search below.

T	E	C	T	M	K	I	S
H	S	P	A	R	R	O	W
R	O	B	I	N	I	O	A
U	E	Z	X	O	E	W	L
S	Z	I	E	T	O	M	L
H	Q	M	Z	E	G	T	O
W	R	E	N	L	I	N	W
A	G	Y	P	L	A	W	Q

October 2004

	school notes/homework	what's on this week
monday **18**	Robbie Savage, 30 today	
tuesday **19**		
wednesday **20**	Claudio Ranieri, 53 today Florent Sinama-Pongelle, 20 today	
thursday **21**		
friday **22**	Arsene Wenger, 55 today	
saturday **23**	Pelé, Brazilian footballer, 64 today	
sunday **24**	Wayne Rooney, 19 today World's first football club, Sheffield FC, is formed, 1857	

FACTS OF THE WEEK

NATURAL CREATIONS

The sea is strong enough to carve into rock! Pounding waves batter coastlines and erode, or wear away, the rock. Sometimes these powerful waves can create amazing shapes such as pillars called sea stacks.

PUNK CULTURE

Punk was a fad of 1970s youth culture and it started a craze for body art that is still popular. Ripped clothes, safety-pin piercings, chains, studs and spiky coloured hair were worn as an expression of freedom and a rebellion against conformity.

SHIPS IN THE SKY

The world's biggest airships were the Hindenberg, destroyed by fire in 1937, and the Graf Zeppelin II, last used in 1940. They were 245 metres long and carried 75 passengers plus 25 crew, gliding almost silently above the oceans.

JOKE OF THE WEEK

"What are Brazilian football fans called?"
"Brazil nuts!"

QUICK QUIZ

1. Which legendary former Man United manager died in 1994?
2. Which country hosted Euro 96?
3. Which country has Luis Figo played for?
4. Who became Brazil's Minister of Sport in 1994?
5. What position does Richard Wright play in?
6. Who was France's top scorer during the 1998 World Cup?

1. Sir Matt Busby 2. England 3. Portugal 4. Pelé 5. Goalkeeper 6. Thierry Henry

ODD SONG OUT

Which song is the odd one out and why?

YESTERDAY, HELP, MY GIRL, LET IT BE

MY GIRL – All the others are by the Beatles

October 2004

	school notes/homework	what's on this week
monday **25**		
tuesday **26**	The English Football Association formed, 1863	
wednesday **27**		
thursday **28**	Milan Baros, 23 today	
friday **29**	Edwin van der Sar, 34 today	
saturday **30**	Muzzy Izzet, 30 today	
sunday **31**		

FACTS OF THE WEEK

INSECT LEAPER

The click beetle is about 12 millimetres long. When in danger it falls on its back and pretends to be dead. But it slowly arches its body  and then straightens with a jerk and a 'click'. It can flick itself about 25 centimetres into the air!

FRIGHTENINGLY FUNNY

Over the centuries, many sinister figures from traditional myths and legends have been turned into pleasant or  harmless characters. For example, the movie Hocus Pocus features three silly, clumsy witches outwitted by a group of children.

PREDICTING THE FUTURE

Roman people were very superstitious. They believed that they could foretell the future by observing animals, birds, insects and even the weather! For example, bees were a sign of riches and happiness but a hooting owl foretold danger.

QUICK QUIZ

1. Which team plays their home games at Deepdale?
2. Which manager was known as Big Ron?
3. Which French striker left Arsenal for Real Madrid in 1994?
4. What colour are Ipswich Town's home shirts?
5. Which former Arsenal player is known as Manu?
6. Which international stadium was famous for its Twin Towers?

1. Preston North End
2. Ron Atkinson
3. Nicolas Anelka 4. Blue
5. Emmanuel Petit 6. Wembley

HALLOWEEN SEARCH

Hidden below are five halloween words for you to find!

```
T R I C K W E C
R C U Q N I O A
E C M U Y K N U
A C O Q P Z N U L
T A K E T U O D
Z Q I J K L L R
P U M P K I N O
W I T C H S X N
```

November 2004

	school notes/homework	what's on this week
monday **1**		
tuesday **2**		
wednesday **3**	Ugo Ehiogu, 32 today	
thursday **4**	Luis Figo, 32 today Mario Melchiot, 28 today	
friday **5**	Bonfire night	
saturday **6**		
sunday **7**	Rio Ferdinand, 26 today	

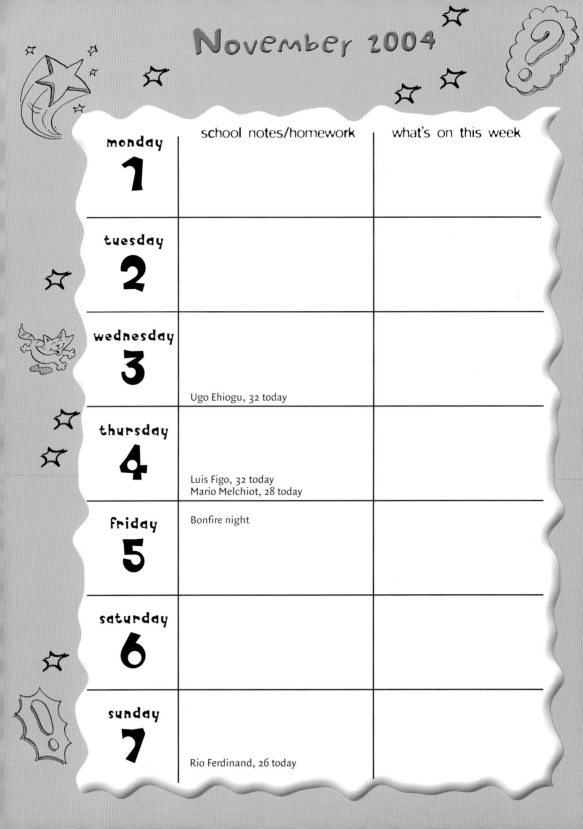

FACTS OF THE WEEK

FROM NORTH TO SOUTH

The spinning Earth acts like a magnet. At the centre of the Earth is liquid iron. As the Earth spins, it makes the iron behave like a magnet with a North and South Pole. These act on the magnet in a compass to make the needle point to the North and South Poles.

MACBETH

Glamis Castle in Scotland is the scene for the play 'Macbeth' by William Shakespeare. In the play, the ambitious Macbeth plots with his evil wife to kill the Scottish king, Duncan, and claim the throne for himself. In real life, Macbeth did defeat and kill Duncan in 1040.

CREATURES EVEN OLDER THAN DINOSAURS!

Dinosaurs were not the first animals on Earth. Many other kinds of creatures lived before them, including many other types of reptiles. Over millions of years one of these groups of reptiles probably changed very slowly, or evolved, into the first dinosaurs.

JOKE OF THE WEEK

"Which football team loves ice cream?"
"Aston Vanilla!"

QUICK QUIZ

1. Which club's ground is at White Hart Lane?
2. Where was the 1996 World Cup final played?
3. What colour do Spain wear for home games?
4. What nationality is Gerard Houllier?
5. Which team are nicknamed the Red Devils?
6. Rio Ferdinand and Les Ferdinand are cousins – true or false?

1. Tottenham Hotspur
2. Wembley Stadium 3. Red
4. French 5. Man United
6. True

WORD SCRAMBLE

Try and guess the BONFIRE NIGHT word in the scramble below!

RESGNAB!

BANGERS!

November 2004

	school notes/homework	what's on this week
monday **8**	Joe Cole, 23 today Aaron Hughes, 27 today	
tuesday **9**	Alessandro del Piero, 30 today	
wednesday **10**	Jens Lehmann, 35 today	
thursday **11**		
friday **12**		
saturday **13**		
sunday **14**		

FACTS OF THE WEEK

SETTING A TRAP

The trapdoor spider lives in a burrow with a wedge-shaped door made from silk. The spider hides just behind this door. When it detects a small animal passing, it opens the door and rushes out to grab its victim.

HE WHO MUST BE OBEYED

A Roman father had the power of life and death over his family. According to Roman law, each family had to be headed by a man. He was known as the 'paterfamilias' (father of a family), and was usually the oldest surviving male.

THE FASTEST SUPERSONIC AIRLINER

Only 16 Concordes were ever built, as a joint project between Britain and France. The world's only commercial supersonic airliner flew at 2,300 km/h, crossing the Atlantic in under three hours. No Concorde had ever crashed until 2000.

JOKE OF THE WEEK

"What is a goalkeeper's favourite snack?"
"Beans on post!"

WORD PUZZLE

Which similar sounding words mean the following?

(a) FIERCE FURRY ANIMAL/NO CLOTHES ON (b) A NEAT PATTERN/AS GOOD AS MONEY

(a) bear/bare (b) check/cheque

November 2004

	school notes/homework	what's on this week
monday **15**		
tuesday **16**	Paul Scholes, 30 today	
wednesday **17**		
thursday **18**		
friday **19**	Pelé scores his 100th goal, 1969	
saturday **20**		
sunday **21**		

FACTS OF THE WEEK

KING ARTHUR AND EXCALIBUR

Legend says that King Arthur became king after pulling a magic sword called Excalibur out of a stone. This act proved that he was the right person to rule Britain. People have written stories about Arthur and the Knights of the Round Table, for more than 1,000 years.

NATURAL RESOURCE

In Iceland, underground steam is used to make lights work. The steam is sent to power stations and is used to work generators to make electricity. The electricity then flows to homes and powers electrical equipment such as lights, televisions and computers.

ITS JUST AND ILLUSION

Flying fish cannot really fly. Fish can't survive out of water, but flying fish sometimes leap above the waves when they are travelling at high speeds. They use their winglike fins to keep them in the air for as long as 30 seconds.

NAME SCRAMBLE

Which popular holiday destination is hidden in these letters?

ZABII

JOKE OF THE WEEK

"How do hens encourage their football teams?"
"They egg them on!"

November 2004

	school notes/homework	what's on this week
monday **22**		
tuesday **23**		
wednesday **24**		
thursday **25**		
friday **26**		
saturday **27**		
sunday **28**		

FACTS OF THE WEEK

NO PADDLING TODAY

Tidal waves are the most powerful waves. Also known as tsunamis, they happen when underwater earthquakes trigger tremendous shock waves. These whip up a wall of water that travels across the sea's surface.

SOUND SYSTEMS

Mole-crickets get their name from the way they tunnel through soil, like real moles. The burrow entrance is specially shaped, almost like the loudspeaker of a music system. It makes the crickets chirps sound louder and travel farther.

THE CHAMPIONS!

The ultimate football prize, the World Cup Trophy is presented to the winning team every four years. Countries qualify for the final stages through an elimination series. Brazil are the only nation to have played in every World Cup finals stage.

JOKE OF THE WEEK

"Why don't grasshoppers go to football matches?"
"They prefer cricket!"

November/December 2004

		school notes/homework	what's on this week
monday	**29**	St. Andrew's Day Ryan Giggs, 31 today	
tuesday	**30**		
wednesday	**1**		
thursday	**2**		
friday	**3**		
saturday	**4**		
sunday	**5**		

FACTS OF THE WEEK

LOOKING OUT FOR FOSSILS

Some fossils look like coiled snakes but are really shellfish called ammonites. An ammonite's body was covered by a spiral shell. The body rotted away leaving the shell to become the fossil. Ammonites lived in the seas at the same time as the dinosaurs lived on land.

WELL BEHAVED

Medieval knights had to behave according to a set of rules, known as the 'code of chivalry'. The code involved being brave and honourable on the battlefield, and treating the enemy politely and fairly. It also instructed knights how to behave towards women.

SQUATTERS' RIGHTS

Most crabs shed their shells as they outgrow them, but the hermit crab does not have a shell. It borrows the leftover shell of a dead whelk or other mollusc – whatever it can squeeze into to protect its soft body.

JOKE OF THE WEEK

"Why did the chicken get a red card?"
"For persistent fowl play!"

QUICK QUIZ

1. Which club sold Lee Bowyer to Leeds?
2. What type of wave became popular during the 1986 World Cup?
3. In which country do Galatasaray play their home matches?
4. In which decade was David Seaman born?
5. In which Italian city is the San Siro Stadium?
6. Which German club play their home matches ar the Olympic Stadium?

1. Charlton Athletic
2. Mexican wave 3. Turkey
4. 1960s 5. Milan
6. Bayern Munich

WORD SEARCH

Can you find the names of five cities below?

```
G C A R D I F F
L C X Z I E S O
A C W Q O I E X
S E T D Z B M F
G Y O R K Z Q O
O C X R U I L R
W D E L Y V X D
B E L F A S T A
```

December 2004

	school notes/homework	what's on this week
monday **6**		
tuesday **7**	John Terry, 24 today	
wednesday **8**		
thursday **9**	Bixente Lizarazu, 35 today	
friday **10**		
saturday **11**		
sunday **12**	Nolberto Solano, 30 today	

FACTS OF THE WEEK

OUT OF ACTION

This gold leaf crab spider has caught a honeybee. Its venom works fast to paralyse the bee. If it did not, the bee's struggling might harm the spider and draw the attention of the spider's enemies.

ANIMAL LOVERS

Roman families liked to keep pets. Roman statues and paintings show many children playing with their pets. Dogs, cats and doves were all popular. Some families also kept ornamental fish and tame deer.

DEAD AS A DODO

The dodo lived undisturbed on the island of Mauritius in the Indian Ocean until European sailors arrived in the 1500s. Sailors killed the birds for food, and rats and cats ate the eggs. By 1680 the dodo was extinct.

JOKE OF THE WEEK

"Why didn't the dog want to play football?"
"Because it was a boxer!"

QUICK QUIZ

1. How is Edson Arantes do Nascimento better known?
2. Which Spanish club won the first five European Cups?
3. In which decade did Wimbledon play their first Football league game?
4. Lazio come from which Italian city?
5. Was the Premier League reduced to 20 teams in 1993 or 1995?
6. With regards to football what is a Christmas tree?

1. Pelé 2. Real Madrid 3. 1970s 4. Rome 5. 1995 6. A playing formation

NAME THE GROUPS

What are groups of the following animals called?

(a) WOLVES (b) GEESE
(c) BEES (d) CROWS
(e) ELEPHANTS

(a) pack (b) gaggle (c) swarm
(d) murder (e) herd

December 2004

	school notes/homework	what's on this week
monday **13**		
tuesday **14**	Michael Owen, 25 today Thomas Radzinski, 31 today	
wednesday **15**		
thursday **16**		
friday **17**		
saturday **18**		
sunday **19**		

FACTS OF THE WEEK

WHAT A WEAPON!

Hammerhead sharks have a hammer-shaped head! With a nostril and an eye on each end of the 'hammer', they swing their head from side to side. This gives them double the chance to see and sniff out any signs of a tasty catch.

REGGAE MUSIC

Reggae is a type of dance music from Jamaica, noted for its use of a heavy offbeat rhythm. It was made world-famous in the 1970s by Bob Marley (1945–81) and his group The Wailers. He had a string of hits before his early death at the age of 34.

FOR A CUP OF TEA

Drinking tea is a strong cultural tradition in many parts of the world – notably Japan, China, India and Britain. In much of Asia, the people who grow and pick the tea are poor workers, while those who enjoy it are rich consumers.

JOKE OF THE WEEK

"Which insect didn't play well in goal?"
"The fumble bee!"

QUICK QUIZ

1. How many corner flags are on a football pitch?
2. Why would a referee move the ball forward 10 yards after giving a free kick?
3. What club are nicknamed the Gills?
4. Who captained England to World Cup glory in 1966?
5. What colour are the home jerseys of Scotland and France?
6. Which club was formed first: Sheffield Wednesday or Sheffield United?

1. Four 2. If defending team show dissent 3. Gillingham 4. Bobby Moore 5. Blue 6. Sheffield United

NAME THE NATIVE

What are the people who live in the following countries called?

(a) SWITZERLAND
(b) MALTA
(c) EGYPT

(a) Swiss (b) Maltese (c) Egyptian

December 2004

	school notes/homework	what's on this week
monday **20**	Geremi Njitap, 26 today Ashley Cole, 24 today	
tuesday **21**	Shortest Day	
wednesday **22**		
thursday **23**		
friday **24**	Christmas Eve	
saturday **25**	Christmas Day	
sunday **26**	Boxing Day	

FACTS OF THE WEEK

NEW SUIT FOR SANTA

The name 'Santa Claus' comes from the Dutch Sinter Klaus, short for Sinter Nikolaus or Saint Nicholas. The traditional outfit for Santa was designed by Coca Cola and first appeared in advertisements in 1931. Before this re-vamp Santa's outfit was green!

MOBILE HOME

Marsupials give birth to tiny young that finish developing in a pouch. A baby kangaroo is only 2 centimetres long when it is born. Tiny, blind and hairless, it makes its own way to the safety of its mother's pouch. Once there, it latches onto a teat in the pouch and begins to feed.

BURIED TREASURE

The Egyptians believed that dead people went on to another life. They filled their dead rulers' tombs with things they might need in the next life. These included jewels and food. This gold mask was found in the tomb of the boy-king Tutankhamun.

JOKE OF THE WEEK

"Why did the footballer hold his boot to his ear?"
"Because he liked sole music!"

WORD SEARCH

Try and find five Christmas delights in the word search below:

```
R C T S A N T A
E Y J W C E O C
I N V E W Z U R
N S V E M U T A
D H O T L Y M C
E E T S B N M K
E H O L L Y M E
R A G J I O M R
```

	school notes/homework	what's on this week
monday **27** David Dunn, 25 today		
tuesday **28** Lomano Lua Lua, 24 today		
wednesday **29** Kieron Dyer, 26 today		
thursday **30**		
friday **31** Sir Alex Ferguson, 63 today		
saturday **1**	New Year's Day Lilian Thuram, 33 today	
sunday **2**		

FACTS OF THE WEEK

SO ATTRACTIVE

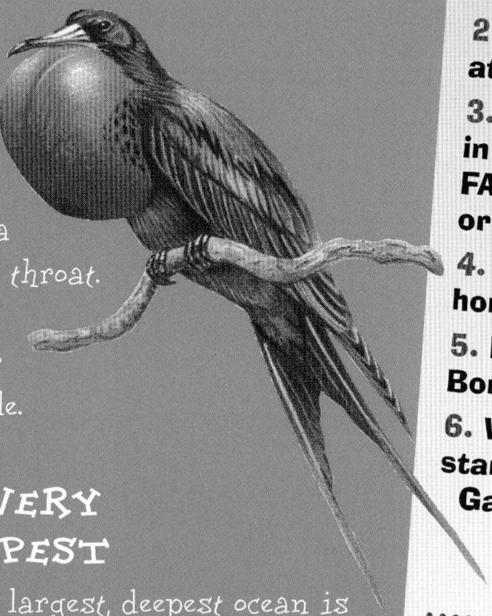

Frigate birds puff up a balloon for their mate. Male frigate birds have a bright-red pouch on their throat. They inflate, or blow up, the pouch as part of their display to attract a female.

THE VERY DEEPEST

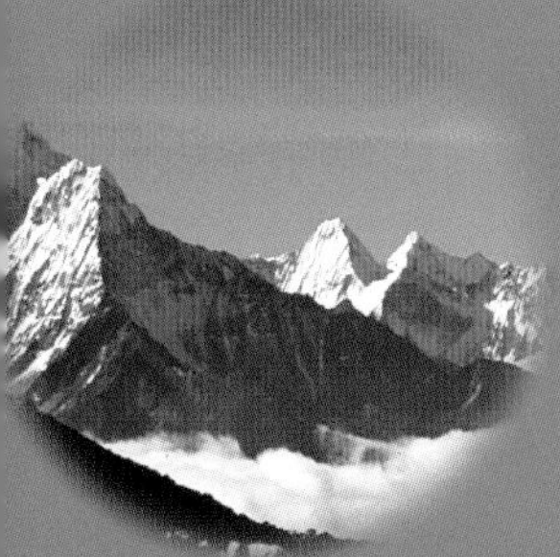

The largest, deepest ocean is the Pacific. It covers nearly half of our planet and is almost as big as the other three oceans put together! In places, the Pacific is so deep that the Earth's tallest mountain, Everest, would sink without a trace.

ROMAN MAKE-UP

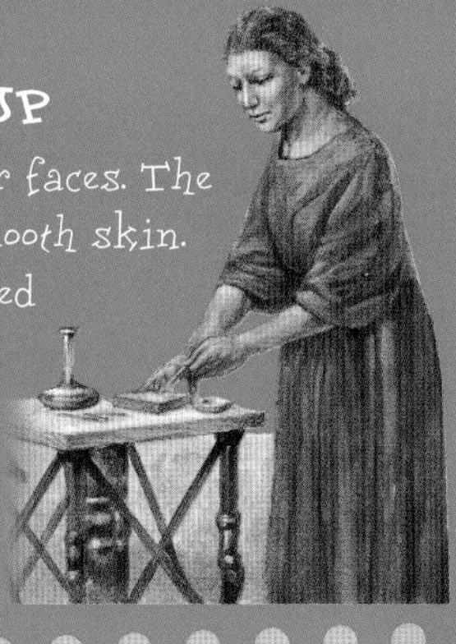

The Romans painted their faces. The Romans admired pale, smooth skin. Women, and some men, used stick-on patches of cloth called 'splenia' to cover spots, and wore lots of make-up.

JOKE OF THE WEEK

"What's a footballer's favourite hot drink?"
"Penaltea!"

QUICK QUIZ

1. What is the only Scottish League team beginning with L?
2. Who was the top scorer at the 2002 World Cup?
3. Dennis Wise was in Wimbledon's 1998 FA Cup-winning side: true or false?
4. Partick Thistle play their home games in which city?
5. In which country does Borussia Dortmund play?
6. Which team do Oasis stars Noel and Liam Gallagher support?

1. Livingston 2. Ronaldo 3. True 4. Glasgow 5. Germany 6. Manchester City

NAME SCRABLE

Which superstar singer is hidden in these letters?

HRIAAM ERYAC

MARIAH CAREY

January 2005

	school notes/homework	what's on this week
monday **3**	Lee Bowyer, 28 today	
tuesday **4**		
wednesday **5**		
thursday **6**	Steed Malbranque, 25 today	
friday **7**		
saturday **8**	Adrian Mutu, 26 today	
sunday **9**		

FACTS OF THE WEEK

BALANCING TRICK

Emperor penguin dads balance an egg on their feet. They do this to keep the egg off the Antarctic ice, where it would freeze. The female leaves her mate with the egg for the whole two months that it takes to hatch.

'CANDLE IN THE WIND'

Elton John rewrote his song 'Candle in the Wind' for the funeral of Princess Diana in 1997. It became the biggest-selling single ever, with worldwide sales of more than 33 million.

RAINING FISH

Storm winds create strong up-draughts of air over water that can suck up fish and frogs. The animals rain down from the sky, to the surprise of people below!

QUICK QUIZ

1. Malmö and Gothenburg are both clubs from which country?
2. Which football team did David Seaman join in 1990 for a then record fee?
3. Which London club were originally called Thames Ironworks FC?
4. In which Spanish city is the Bernabeu Stadium?
5. Which Italian club won the UEFA Cup in 1999?
6. Which two Scottish teams make up the Old Firm?

1. Sweden 2. Arsenal 3. West Ham 4. Madrid 5. Parma 6. Celtic and Rangers

ODD ONE OUT

Which one of the four is the ODD ONE OUT and, why?

SPROUT, POTATO, TOMATO, ONION

TOMATO – all the others are vegetables

January 2005

	school notes/homework	what's on this week
monday **10**		
tuesday **11**	Emile Heskey, 27 today	
wednesday **12**		
thursday **13**		
friday **14**		
saturday **15**	El Hadji Diouf, 24 today	
sunday **16**		

FACTS OF THE WEEK

REACH FOR THE REPELLENT

Blood-sucking flies bite a person with a certain disease, such as malaria, and suck in a small amount of blood. This contains microscopic germs which cause the disease. As the fly bites another person – the disease is passed on.

SO CLEVER

There are gemstones under the sea. Pearls are made by oysters. If a grain of sand is lodged inside an oyster's shell, it irritates its soft body. The oyster coats the sand with a substance called nacre, over the years, more nacre builds up and the pearl gets bigger.

ANTARCTIC DISASTER

Captain Robert Scott's second expedition to reach the South Pole ended in tragedy. When his team finally reached the South Pole on January 18, 1912, they found that a Norwegian team had arrived there one month earlier. Scott and his men died from hunger and the cold on the way home.

QUICK QUIZ

1. How old was Wayne Rooney when he first scored for England?
2. Which high profile manager acquired the nickname El Tel?
3. What is the last name of Scottish club Forfar?
4. Is the middle name of Emile Heskey: Lancelot or Ivanhoe?
5. Are St Mirren nicknamed The Pals or The Buddies?
6. In how many World Cups did Pelé score?

1. 17 years and 317 days
2. Terry Venables
3. Athletic 4. Ivanhoe
5. The Buddies 6. Two

PROVERBIAL PUZZLE

In the proverb, what do too many cooks spoil?

January 2005

	school notes/homework	what's on this week
monday **17**		
tuesday **18**		
wednesday **19**	Lauren, 28 today	
thursday **20**	Owen Hargreaves, 24 today	
friday **21**	Phil Neville, 28 today Nicky Butt, 30 today Jonathan Woodgate, 25 today	
saturday **22**		
sunday **23**		

FACTS OF THE WEEK

SUPERSTAR

American actor Brad Pitt is one of the most popular film stars of modern times. Newspapers often encourage readers to think that the lives of such superstars are as dramatic as the mythical characters they portray on screen.

DEEP SEA DIVER

In 1960, two men inside the diving vehicle 'Trieste' descended more than 10 kilometres into the Marianas Trench, the deepest part of the Pacific Ocean. The 'Trieste' was also use to explore the wreck of the Titanic and reclaim some of her contents.

BEHEADED!

Throughout history, people have sometimes turned against their king. Charles I was king of England and Scotland in the 1600s. Although he lost a civil war in Britain, Charles still refused to give up his powers. He was finally beheaded in London on January 31, 1649.

JOKE OF THE WEEK
"Where do spiders play their FA Cup final?"
"Webley stadium!"

QUICK QUIZ

1. Which club are know as The Tractor Boys?
2. Man Utd and Man City have both won which European trophy?
3. Which Premiership club has a cannon on its badge?
4. What position does Wayne Rooney play?
5. In football, what do the initials OG stand for?
6. Who is the youngest person to be appointed a manager of England?

1. Ipswich Town 2. European Cup-Winners Cup 3. Arsenal 4. Striker 5. Own Goal 6. Glenn Hoddle

NAME SCRAMBLE

Which famous home is hidden in the scramble below?

CIGMAHNKUB CELAAP

BUCKINGHAM PALACE

January 2005

	school notes/homework	what's on this week
monday **24**		
tuesday **25**		
wednesday **26**		
thursday **27**		
friday **28**	Gianluigi Buffon, 27 today Jamie Carragher, 27 today	
saturday **29**	Robert Pires, 32 today	
sunday **30**		

FACTS OF THE WEEK

LITTLE CHANGE

Roman combs were made from bone, ivory or wood. Like combs today, they were designed to smooth and untangle hair, and were sometimes worn as hair ornaments. But they had another, less pleasant, purpose – they were used for combing out all the little nits and lice!

THE SMALLEST AND THE TALLEST

One of the smallest mammals is a bat. It is called Kitti's hog-nosed bat and is less than 2 centimetres long – about the same size as a bumble bee. The tallest mammal is the giraffe measuring a mighty 5.5 metres high.

CHANGING SHAPE

The Moon seems to change shape from day to day. It takes 28.73 days to pass through all these changes, which we call phases. Sometimes we see just a tiny slice of the Moon – this is because the rest of the Moon is in darkness.

JOKE OF THE WEEK

"Why do managers take suitcases to football games?"
"So that they can pack the defence!"

January/February 2005

	school notes/homework	what's on this week
monday **31**		
tuesday **1**		
wednesday **2**	Barry Ferguson, 27 today	
thursday **3**		
friday **4**		
saturday **5**	Christiano Ronaldo, 20 today	
sunday **6**		

FACTS OF THE WEEK

MEDIEVAL FIGHTING

Jousting was introduced because so many knights were being killed or wounded during tournaments. Jousting was a fight between two knights on horseback. Each knight tried to win by knocking the other off his horse.

HIDDEN TREASURES

There is treasure lying under the sea. Over the centuries, many ships sunk in storms or hit reefs. They include pirate ships loaded with stolen booty. The bed of the Caribbean Sea is littered with the remains of Spanish galleons, many of which still hold treasure!

THE BIG APPLE

Broadway in New York is America's theatreland – the equivalent of London's West End – and is the place were British and American actors most want to perform. If a play transfers to Broadway from a West End theatre, it is considered a success.

JOKE OF THE WEEK

"Why did the football players sketch crockery?"
"It was a cup draw!"

WORD SEARCH

Try and find five boys or girls names in the word search below

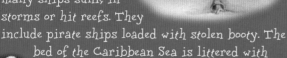

```
L K T T X W A M
E V O P O D C I
S E N Q N U Y C
L P Y C B Y R H
E C W Y I O P E
Y A Q Y J M B L
S K E L L Y U L
T E R R Y Y R E
```

February 2005

	school notes/homework	what's on this week
monday **7**		
tuesday **8**		
wednesday **9**		
thursday **10**	Salif Diao, 28 today	
friday **11**		
saturday **12**		
sunday **13**		

FACTS OF THE WEEK

DON'T TRY THIS AT HOME

Sauropod dinosaurs may have swallowed pebbles – on purpose! Their peglike *teeth* could only rake in plant food, not chew it. Pebbles and *stones* gulped into the stomach helped to grind and crush the food.

EARLY ROMANCE

The Romans invented Valentine's Day, but called it Lupercalia. Boys picked a girl's name from a hat, and she was meant to be their girlfriend for the year! Childhood was short for a Roman girl. Roman law allowed girls to get married at 12 years old.

DRAMATIC THEATRE

The Colosseum was a vast amphitheatre in Rome, Italy. Ancient Romans flocked there – it held up to 50,000 spectators – to watch gladiators fighting each other or wild animals. There was even a mock sea battle in the arena, which was flooded for the occasion.

QUICK QUIZ

1. What number shirt did Eric Cantona wear at Old Trafford?
2. What is the last name of Scottish club Raith?
3. Can an attacking player be offside in his own half?
4. What does the U stand for in UEFA?
5. Who is older: Joe Cole or Ashley Cole?
6. Which club play their home games at the Abbey Stadium?

1. 7 2. Rovers 3. No 4. Union 5. Ashley Cole 6. Cambridge United

COCKNEY LINGO

What words do the following Cockney Rhymes describe?

(a) Apples and pears (b) North and south (c) Plates of meat (d) Dog and bone (e) Trouble and strife

(a) stairs (b) mouth (c) feet (d) phone (e) wife

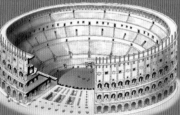

JOKE OF THE WEEK

"Why did the struggling manager shake the club cat?"
"To see if there was any more money in the kitty!"

February 2005

	school notes/homework	what's on this week
monday **14**	Kevin Keegan, 54 today	
tuesday **15**		
wednesday **16**		
thursday **17**		
friday **18**	Gary Neville, 30 today Bobby Robson, 72 today	
saturday **19**		
sunday **20**		

FACTS OF THE WEEK

A TERRIBLE END

In the 1420s a young French girl called Joan of Arc led the French army against the English, who had surrounded the city of Orléans. After ten

days the English were defeated. Joan was later captured, accused of being a witch, and burned to death.

ESSENTIAL EQUIPMENT

Divers have a spare pair of lungs. Scuba divers wear special breathing apparatus called 'aqua lungs'. French

divers, Jacques Cousteau and Emile Gagnan, came up with the idea of a portable oxygen supply.

THE WONDER DRUG TO TREAT INFECTIONS

In 1928 Alexander Fleming found that penicillin mould, killed bacteria – a chance discovery that led to the first antibiotic, penicillin. It is prescribed by doctors to treat all sorts of infections.

JOKE OF THE WEEK
"Where do football directors go when they are fed up?"
"The bored room!"

WORD SCRAMBLE

Scrambled in the mix-up below is a famous football player!

HICMEAL NEOW

MICHAEL OWEN

February 2005

	school notes/homework	what's on this week
monday **21**		
tuesday **22**		
wednesday **23**		
thursday **24**		
friday **25**		
saturday **26**	Ole Gunnar Solskjaer, 32 today	
sunday **27**	James Beattie, 27 today	

FACTS OF THE WEEK

EARLY BIRD

Birds first appeared about 150 million years ago. It is possible that over millions of years certain small, meat-eating dinosaurs called raptors developed feathers. Slowly their arms became wings. Gradually they evolved into the very first birds.

FOR THE FUTURE

The planned Freedom Ship will resemble a floating city. It will be one of the first ocean cities, with apartments, shopping centres, a school and a hospital. The people who live on Freedom will circle the Earth once every two years. By following the Sun, they will live in constant summertime!

MIRACLE BABY

Louise Brown, born in 1978, was the first 'test-tube' baby. She was conceived outside her mothers's body, and the fertilized egg was then implanted in her mothers's womb to continue growing normally.

JOKE OF THE WEEK

Manager to player: "What happened to the three week diet?"
Player to Manager: "I finished it in three days!"

QUICK QUIZ

1. What is the home ground of Nottingham Forest?
2. Is Bobby Robson is the uncle of Bryan Robson?
3. How old was Michael Owen when he played for England in his first World Cup?
4. David Beckham was born in Brooklyn: true or false?
5. What is the last name of Scottish club Ross?
6. In the 2000–01 season who was leading scorer for Leeds?

1. City Ground 2. No 3. 18 4. False, he was born in London 5. City 6. Mark Viduka

PROVERBIAL PUZZLE

In the proverb, red sky at night is shepherd's delight, but red sky in the morning is what?

Shepherd's warning

February/March 2005

	school notes/homework	what's on this week
monday **28**		
tuesday **1**	St David's Day	
wednesday **2**	Damien Duff, 26 today	
thursday **3**	Roy Makay, 30 today	
friday **4**		
saturday **5**		
sunday **6**	Tim Howard, 26 today	

FACTS OF THE WEEK

PRAYERS BEFORE DINNER

One of the most powerful insect predators is the preying mantis. It is also called the praying mantis since it holds its front legs folded, like a person with hands together in prayer. But the front legs have sharp spines that snap together to grab caterpillars, moths and similar food.

LOSING COUNT

The worlds's oldest person is usually a woman aged between 110 and 120. Only one person in five over 100 is a man. Many claims for 'oldest person' are false. In 1933 a Chinese man was reported to have died at the age of 233!

ANCIENT MONUMENT

Stonehenge is the most famous ancient monument in Britain. It was built between about 2950 and 1500BC. The huge stones were put up in stages, in three circles that made a giant calendar which was used to fix days for religious ceremonies.

JOKE OF THE WEEK

"Why did the footballer burp during the game?"
"It was a freak hic!"

QUICK QUIZ

1. What did Liverpool win on a golden goal in 2001?

2. What is the name of Sunderland Football Club's stadium?

3. If the ball hits a referee on the way into the net is it a goal?

4. Atalanta is a football club from which country?

5. How many goals did Gary Lineker score at the 1986 Word Cup: 6, 7 or 8?

6. What is the P name of Celtic's home ground?

1. UEFA Cup 2. The Stadium of Light 3. Yes 4. Italy 5. 6 6. Parkhead

NAME SCRAMBLE

Which tall London building is hiding in the scramble below?

RYNAAC FHARW

CANARY WHARF

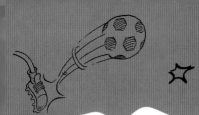

March 2005

	school notes/homework	what's on this week
monday **7**	Ray Parlour, 32 today	
tuesday **8**		
wednesday **9**	Juan Sebastian Veron, 30 today	
thursday **10**		
friday **11**		
saturday **12**		
sunday **13**	Edgar Davids, 32 today	

FACTS OF THE WEEK

SPOOKY HAPPENINGS

Many castles are said to be haunted by the ghosts of people who died within their walls. Edward II of England was murdered in his cell at Berkeley Castle, and visitors to the castle say they can hear the screams of the murdered Edward at night.

KILLING FOR SPORT

Roman gladiators fought wild beasts, as well as each other. Fierce wild animals were brought from distant parts of the Roman empire to be killed by gladiators in the arenas in Rome. So many lions were taken from North Africa that they became extinct there.

MYTHS AND LEGENDS

Mermaids lured sailors to their deaths on the rocks. Mythical mermaids were said to be half-woman, half-fish. Folklore tells how the mermaids confused sailors with their beautiful singing – with the result that their ships were wrecked on the rocks.

QUICK QUIZ

1. Which is the only Scottish city to have staged the European Cup Final?
2. In what year were substitutes first used in the World Cup: 1970 or 1974?
3. Which Club Champions play in the World Club Cup?
4. In what year was David Beckham born?
5. What is the full name of Airdrie?
6. Which player was sold of £48 million by Juventus in 2001?

1. Glasgow 2. 1970 3. European & South American 4. 1975 5. Airdrieonians 6. Zinedine Zidane

WHO IS SHE?

She is my father's niece, my uncle's daughter, and my cousin's sister. Who is she?

My cousin

JOKE OF THE WEEK

"When fish play football, who is the captain?"
"The team's kipper!"

March 2005

	school notes/homework	what's on this week
monday **14**	Nicolas Anelka, 26 today	
tuesday **15**		
wednesday **16**	The first football cup final was played, Kensington Oval, 1872	
thursday **17**	St Patrick's Day	
friday **18**	Danny Murphy, 28 today	
saturday **19**	Alessandro Nesta, 29 today Kolo Toure, 24 today	
sunday **20**		

FACTS OF THE WEEK

WRAPPED IN LAYERS

The Earth is wrapped in layers of gases called the atmosphere. The weather takes place in the lowest layer, the troposphere. The layer above is the  stratosphere. The mesosphere is the middle layer and above it is the thermosphere. The exosphere is about 700 kilometres above your head!

WITCHCRAFT

Despite their advanced technology, Romans believed that illness was caused by witchcraft. To find a cure, they gave presents to the witch, begging her to remove the spell, or made a special visit to a temple, to ask the gods to make them better.

ELEMENTARY MY DEAR WATSON

The most famous detective in literature is Sherlock Holmes. Frequently mistaken by readers for a real person, Holmes and his friend Dr Watson first appeared in Arthur Conan Doyle's story 'A Study In Scarlet'ß in 1887.

QUICK QUIZ

1. Who won the last FA Cup final held at Wembley?
2. In what year did the Millennium Stadium host its first FA Cup Final?
3. When did Pele retire?
4. Which country won the 1998 football World Cup?
5. If you are shown a red card by a referee are you being sent off the pitch or given an official warning?
6. How much did Real Madrid pay for David Beckham in 2003: £25 million or £35 million?

6. £25 million
5. Being sent off
3. 1977 4. France
1. Chelsea 2. 2001

CONUNDRUM

As I was going to St Ives, I met a man with seven wives, each wife had seven sacks, each sack had seven cats, each cat had seven kits; Kits, cats, sacks and wives, How many were going to St Ives?

One, all the others were going back!

JOKE OF THE WEEK

"Why do birds sell quickly on the football transfer market?"
"They tend to go cheep!"

March 2005

	school notes/homework	what's on this week
monday **21**	Ronaldinho, 25 today	
tuesday **22**	The English Football League was founded, 1888	
wednesday **23**	Jerzy Dudek, 32 today	
thursday **24**		
friday **25**		
saturday **26**		**2006 FIFA World Cup™** England v Northern Ireland Wales v Austria Scotland v Italy Republic of Ireland v Israel
sunday **27**	Gaizka Mendieta, 31 today Jimmy Floyd Hasselbaink, 33 today	

FACTS OF THE WEEK

TOP OF THE POPS

Dolphins and whales sing songs to communicate. The noisiest is the humpback whale, whose wailing noises can be heard for hundreds of kilometres. The sweetest is the beluga - nicknamed the 'sea canary'. Songs are used to attract a mate, or just to keep track of each other.

ALL DRIED UP

The driest place on Earth is the Atacama Desert in Chile, South America. Intervals between showers may be as long as 100 years, and in some areas it has not rained for more than 400 years!

WHAT THE DICKENS

Charles Dickens (1812-70) was one of the most popular novelists of all time. His books such as 'A Christmas Carol' and 'Oliver Twist' are full of memorable characters, humour and sadness.

JOKE OF THE WEEK

"How do you stop squirrels playing football?"
"Hide the ball, it drives them nuts!"

QUICK QUIZ

1. In which city was Robbie Fowler born: Birmingham, Liverpool or Leeds?
2. Who was sacked as Spurs manager in 2003?
3. Who do Stoke play in the Potteries Derby?
4. Which Premiership club has a cannon on its badge?
5. Who used to play their home games at Roker Park?
6. Which Premiership star was born Ryan Wilson?

. . . .

1. Liverpool 2. Glenn Hoddle 3. Port Vale 4. Arsenal 5. Sunderland 6. Ryan Giggs

WORD SEARCH

Find the five football clubs hidden below.

```
T H U W S M O A
A E V E R T O N
R E Q S K U E F
S C W T I I S P
E G G H X R P L
N N S A V H U E
A B C M P I R H
L E E D S O S W
```

March/April 2005

	school notes/homework	what's on this week
monday **28**		
tuesday **29**	Rui Costa, 33 today	
wednesday **30**		**2006 FIFA World Cup™** England v Azerbaijan Wales v Austria Northern Ireland v Poland
thursday **31**		
friday **1**	Clarence Seedorf, 29 today	
saturday **2**		
sunday **3**		

FACTS OF THE WEEK

GEORGE AND THE DRAGON

The legend of St George tells how the brave knight killed a fierce dragon. The dragon was terrorizing the people of Lydia. St George arrived and said he would kill their dragon if they became Christians like him. Thousands accepted his offer, and George killed the dragon.

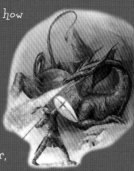

IN ANCIENT ROME

Roman theatres were huge, well-built structures. One of the best-preserved is at Orange, in France. It has seats for almost 10,000 people. It was so cleverly designed that the audience could hear the actors, even from the back row.

BESTSELLING AUTHOR

The biggest-selling writer ever is Agatha Christie (1890–1976). Her 78 crime stories, featuring detectives Hercule Poirot and Miss Marple, have been translated into more than 44 languages. Many have been made into plays.

JOKE OF THE WEEK

"Why did the big cats' team get lots of red cards?"
"They were all cheetahs!"

CAN YOU GUESS?

What are the five largest countries in the world?

April 2005

	school notes/homework	what's on this week
monday **4**		
tuesday **5**	John Hartson, 30 today	
wednesday **6**		
thursday **7**		
friday **8**		
saturday **9**	Robbie Fowler, 30 today	
sunday **10**	Roberto Carlos, 32 today Mario Stanic, 33 today	

FACTS OF THE WEEK

MINOTAUR

The Minotaur was a monster of ancient Greek legend. It had the body of a man, but the head, horns, and tail of a bull, and it fed on human flesh. The Minotaur was kept beneath the palace of King Minos of Crete and was eventually killed by the hero-prince Theseus.

ANCIENT CULTURE

The Roma people – sometimes called 'Gypsies' – have preserved their ancient nomadic way of life for hundreds of years, along with their own customs. Originally from India, Roma now live in many parts of Europe and northern Africa.

CINEMATOGRAPHE

The Lumiere brothers invented the 'cinematographe', a device that combines the camera and the projector. By showing numerous pictures one after the other they could create the illusion of motion.

ODD ONE OUT

Which of these singers is the odd one out?

Madonna, Michael Jackson, Britney Spears, Robbie Williams

Robbie Williams, All the others are American.

JOKE OF THE WEEK

"Why are football grounds odd?"
"Because you can sit in the stands but can't stand in the sits!"

April 2005

	school notes/homework	what's on this week
monday **11** Matt Holland, 31 today		
tuesday **12**		
wednesday **13**		
thursday **14** James McFadden, 22 today		
friday **15**		
saturday **16** Freddie Ljungberg, 28 today		
sunday **17**		

FACTS OF THE WEEK

PAINTBALL BATTLE

The bombardier beetle squirts out a spray of horrible liquid from its rear end, almost like a small spray-gun! This startles and stings the attacker and gives the small beetle time to escape.

BUILT BY THE CONQUEROR

English kings and queens have lived at Windsor Castle since William the Conqueror began building it more than 900 years ago. William's original castle consisted of a wooden fort. The first stone buildings were added in the 1100s.

ALL IN THE DOTS

Braille is a raised-dot alphabet used by blind people. It is read by running the fingertips over the dots, or bumps. Braille was invented by a blind French teenager named Louis Braille in the 1820s.

JOKE OF THE WEEK

"What do you get if you drop a piano on a team's defence?"
"A flat back four!"

QUICK QUIZ

1. Which club's fanzine is called The Flashing Blade?

2. Which nation won the first Women's Football World Cup?

3. From which club did Sunderland buy Marcus Stewart?

4. Who was the first player to score 200 goals in the Premiership?

5. Which club did Gordon Strachan leave to manager Southampton?

6. Who was the manager of Leicester City at the start of the 2003/04 season?

....

1. Sheffield United 2. USA 3. Ipswich Town 4. Alan Shearer 5. Coventry City 6. Micky Adams

WORD SCRAMBLE

Unscramble the letters to find three famous cities

LIBREN, SPAIR, BREENMOUL,

BERLIN, PARIS, MELBOURNE

April 2005

	school notes/homework	what's on this week
monday **18**		
tuesday **19**	Jussi Jaaskelainen, 30 today	
wednesday **20**	Steve Finnan, 29 today Shay Given, 29 today	
thursday **21**		
friday **22**		
saturday **23**	St George's Day	
sunday **24**		

FACTS OF THE WEEK

HURRICANE FORCE

A hurricane is a destructive storm which gathers over a warm part of the ocean. Water evaporating from the ocean forms a vast cloud. As cool air rushes in below the cloud, it turns like a huge spinning wheel. The centre of the hurricane (the eye) is completely still.

OSTRICH DINOSAUR

Struthiomimus was one of the fastest of all the dinosaurs. It was more than 2 metres tall and 4 metres long. It had very long back legs and large clawed feet, like an ostrich. It could probably run at more than 70 kilometres per hour.

WARRIORS FROM THE EAST

Warrior knights in Japan in the Middle Ages were known as Samurai. A long curving sword was a samurai warrior's most treasured possession. Samurai warriors wore armour on the bodies, arms and legs, a helmet and often a crest made up of a pair of horns.

JOKE OF THE WEEK

"Why did the goal post get angry?"
"Because the bar was rattled!"

NUMBER PUZZLE

Multiply the number of legs on a spider by the number of blind mice in the song. Take away the number of the dwarves in Snow White. What is your answer?

17. 8 (legs on a spider) x 3 (blind mice) = 24-7 (dwarves) = 17

April/May 2005

	school notes/homework	what's on this week
monday **25**		
tuesday **26**		
wednesday **27**		
thursday **28**		
friday **29**		
saturday **30**	John O'Shea, 24 today	
sunday **1**		

FACTS OF THE WEEK

BATHTIME PETS

Sponges are animals! They are very simple creatures that filter food from sea water. The natural sponge that you might use in the bath is a long-dead, dried-out sponge.

EARLY CHRISTIANITY

Some of the world's first Christians lived in Rome. But until AD313 Christianity was banned in the Roman Empire. Christians met secretly in underground passages called catacombs, to say prayers and hold services. They also used the catacombs as a burial place.

MAKING MUSIC

The guitar's origins go back to ancient Egypt, but the shape of the Spanish acoustic guitar, shown here, dates from the 1800s. Most guitars have 6 strings, but some have 12. Guitars used by ex-rock stars sell for huge sums of money.

ODD ONE OUT

Which of the following countries is the odd one out and why?

INDIA, JAPAN, KENYA, CHINA

KENYA – All the others are countries in Asia.

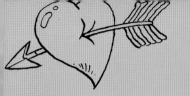

May 2005

	school notes/homework	what's on this week
monday **2**	David Beckham, 30 today Chris Kirkland, 24 today	
tuesday **3**		
wednesday **4**	Eric Djemba-Djemba, 24 today	
thursday **5**		
friday **6**		
saturday **7**		
sunday **8**		

FACTS OF THE WEEK

SAVE THE PLANET!

We can make materials last longer by recycling them. Metal, glass and plastic are thrown away after they have been used, buried in tips and never used again. Today more people recycle materials. This means sending them back to factories to be used again.

WELL ARMED

The narwhal has a horn like a unicorn's. This Arctic whale has a long, twirly tooth which measures about 3 metres long and spirals out of its head. The males use their tusks as a weapon when they are fighting over females.

RIP VAN WINKLE

In the traditional tale, Rip Van Winkle falls into a deep sleep for 20 years. When he finally wakes up, he can't understand why the world is so different.

JOKE OF THE WEEK

"What part of a football ground is never the same?"
"The changing rooms!"

TAKE FIVE

Name the last five different countries to win the football World Cup

Brazil, France, West Germany, Argentina, Italy

May 2005

	school notes/homework	what's on this week
monday **9**	Don Hutchinson, 34 today	
tuesday **10**	Dennis Bergkamp, 36 today Sylvain Wiltord, 31 today	
wednesday **11**		
thursday **12**	Millennium Stadium hosts its first FA Cup Final, 2001	
friday **13**		
saturday **14**		
sunday **15**	Edu, 27 today	

FACTS OF THE WEEK

NO DRIFTING OFF

Sea otters anchor themselves when they sleep. These playful creatures live off the Pacific coast among huge forests of giant seaweed called kelp. When they take a snooze, they wrap a strand of kelp around their body to stop them being washed out to sea.

POISONED QUEEN

Cleopatra was queen of ancient Egypt when the country was under the control of the Romans. She was a very ambitious and determined queen.

According to legend, Cleopatra killed herself by letting a poisonous snake bite her arm.

SAVING THE TREES

For many New Age sympathizers, protecting the natural environment from destruction has become a spiritual quest. They hold ceremonies to celebrate nature's beauty, and campaign to save fragile environments, such as rainforests, from harm.

JOKE OF THE WEEK

"What should a football team do if the pitch is flooded?"
"Bring on their subs!"

QUICK QUIZ

1. David Beckham is older than Ronaldo: true or false?
2. Steven Gerrard was born in the same year as Kieran Dyer: true or false?
3. In what year did Gary Lineker last play as England Captain: 1982 or 1992?
4. How old was Dino Zoff when he played for Italy in the 1982 World Cup?
5. Was Fabien Barthez born in 1971 or 1981?
6. Who did Uruguay beat to win the first ever World Cup final in 1930: Argentina, Italy or Brazil?

1. True 2. False
3. 1992 4. 40 years old
5. 1971 6. Argentina

WORD SEARCH

Can you find five African animals hiding among the letters below?

```
H G I R A F F E
U A D T V E E N
W Z E B R A K O
T E S T C Y R A
J L L R O U H D
N L K E A I I P
S E F J R T N A
B B H I P P O N
```

 # May 2005

	school notes/homework	what's on this week
monday **16**		
tuesday **17**		
wednesday **18**	Danny Mills, 28 today Brad Friedel, 34 today	
thursday **19**	Diego Forlan, 26 today	
friday **20**	Last FA Cup Final held at Wembley Stadium, 2000	
saturday **21**	Laurent Robert, 30 today Quinton Fortune, 28 today	
sunday **22**		

FACTS OF THE WEEK

IVANHOE

Ivanhoe was a medieval knight who lived in the time of Richard the Lionheart. He is the hero of a historical book called 'Ivanhoe', written by the Scottish novelist Sir Walter Scott in the 1800s, and describes the conflict between the Saxon people and their Norman conquerors.

SIGNS OF FAITH

Some Jewish men wear special clothes as a sign of their faith. The kippah (or yarmulke) is a little cap that covers the crown of the head and is worn as a mark of respect for God. For praying, Jewish men may wear a tallit, or shawl.

THE LOUVRE

The Louvre in Paris contains one of the world's greatest art collections. Once a royal palace, it was extended in the 17th century to house the growing royal collection. In 1989 it was given a new, ultramodern entrance under a pyramid.

QUICK QUIZ

1. ECHOES ALLY is an anagram of which player?
2. At the 2002 Olympic Games which nation won the Men's Football gold medal?
3. Which football player is older: Paul Scholes or Rio Ferdinand?
4. What became the new home ground of Manchester City in 2003?
5. Who sold his controlling shares is Chelsea FC in July 2003?
6. What did Sunderland change their nickname to after leaving Roker Park?

1. Ashley Cole 2. Cameroon 3. Paul Scholes 4. The City of Manchester Stadium 5. Ken Bates 6. The Black Cats

NUMBER PUZZLE

Which number should replace the question mark?

8	7	6	9	?
3	5	4	6	5
5	2	2	3	9

Answer: 14

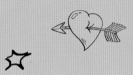

May 2005

	school notes/homework	what's on this week
monday **23**		
tuesday **24**	Vladimir Smicer, 32 today	
wednesday **25**		
thursday **26**		
friday **27**		
saturday **28**		
sunday **29**		

FACTS OF THE WEEK

IN THE PINK

Walruses seem to change colour! When a walrus is in the water, it appears pale brown or even white. This is because blood drains from the skin's surface to stop the body losing heat. On land, the blood returns to the skin and walruses can look reddish brown or pink!

SUPERSTARDOM

Madonna, born Madonna Louise Ciccone, burst into the pop scene in 1984 with her Album Like a Virgin. She became the biggest-selling female singer in showbiz history. Her string of over 40 hits have made more than 100 million sales.

GULLIVER'S TRAVELS

The fantasy-adventure story about Gulliver in the lands of miniature people and giants, by the British author Jonathan Swift (1667–1745), is a witty satire on human foolishness, It mocks the words and deeds of politicians, scientists and philosophers.

JOKE OF THE WEEK
"What do you call the goalie in a ladies' team?"
"Annette!"

QUICK QUIZ

1. Robert Pires was born in Jamaica: true or false?
2. Who cost Liverpool more – Harry Kewell or El Hadji Diouf?
3. What nationality is Raul?
4. INCOME WHALE is an anagram of which player?
5. How long is a regular football match?
6. Hernan Crespo plays international football for which country?

1. False 2. El Hadji Diouf 3. Spanish 4. Michael Owen 5. 90 minutes 6. Argentina

ODD ONE OUT

Which of these stands out like a sore thumb and why?

MOSCOW, MADRID, ROME, MUNICH

MUNICH – All the others are European capital cities.

May/June 2005

	school notes/homework	what's on this week
monday **30**	Steven Gerrard, 25 today	
tuesday **31**		
wednesday **1**		
thursday **2**		
friday **3**		
saturday **4**		**2006 FIFA World Cup™** Scotland v Moldova Republic of Ireland v Israel
sunday **5**		

FACTS OF THE WEEK

OFF INTO BATTLE

Insects have some of the best types of camouflage in the whole world of animals Shieldbugs have broad, flat bodies that look like the leaves around them. The body is shaped like the shield carried by a medieval knight-in-armour.

RADIO ENTERTAINMENT

The radio was invented by the Italian Guglielmo Marconi in 1894 at his electronics company in Chelmsford, Essex.
At first it was designed only to transmit simple messages but in 1906 music was broadcast.

COSSACK DANCER

A Cossack dancer from Ukraine leaps high in the air, showing off his agility. Cossacks were famous for their bravery and horse riding skills, and the men traditionally expressed their warlike energy in dramatic dances.

MIND PUZZLE

How many pieces are there on a chess board at the start of a game?

June 2005

	school notes/homework	what's on this week
monday **6**		
tuesday **7**		
wednesday **8**		**2006 FIFA World Cup™** Scotland v Belarus Republic of Ireland v Faroe Islands
thursday **9**		
friday **10**		
saturday **11**		
sunday **12**	Thomas Sorensen, 29 today	

FACTS OF THE WEEK

BABY FATHERS

Seahorse dads have the babies. They don't exactly give birth, but they store the eggs in a pouch on their belly. When the eggs are ready to hatch, a stream of miniature seahorses billows out from the dad's pouch.

SOUND RECORDINGS

The first gramophone, called a phonograph, was produced by the American inventor Thomas Alva Edison in 1878. It used cylinders to record and play sounds. Ten years later the first flat disc was introduced. A needle picked up the sound from grooves in the disc.

A MODERN SAINT?

Diana, Princess of Wales (1961-97), became famous for the work she did to help people who were ill, injured or outcast. Some people called her a 'modern saint'. But religious leaders did not approve of this title.

June 2005

	school notes/homework	what's on this week
monday **13**		
tuesday **14**		
wednesday **15**	Oliver Kahn, 36 today	
thursday **16**		
friday **17**	Gary Lineker plays his last match as England captain, 1982	
saturday **18**		
sunday **19**	M Cafu, 35 today Kleberson, 26 today	

FACTS OF THE WEEK

THE EARTH IS NEARLY 5 BILLION YEARS OLD!

From a ball of molten rock Earth has changed into a living, breathing planet. We must try to keep it that way. Switching off lights to save energy and picking up litter are small things we can all do.

DINOSAUR NESTS

Like most reptiles today, dinosaurs produced young by laying eggs. These hatched out into baby dinosaurs which gradually grew into adults. Fossils have been found of eggs with dinosaurs still developing inside, as well as fossils of just-hatched baby dinosaurs.

PLAYING GOD?

Dolly the sheep was born in Scotland in 1997. Created by scientists using genetic engineering techniques, she was the first mammal to be cloned (copied) from adult cells. Some people fear that scientists are starting to copy God's role of creator.

JOKE OF THE WEEK

"Football players are the only people who can dribble and still look cool!"

WORD SEARCH

Can you find the names of five vegetables hidden below?

```
H P O T A T O X
U A D T V E E T
W T U R N I P U
T L E E K Y R R
J F L R O U H N
S P I N A C H G
S E F J R T N P
C A R R O T Z N
```

June 2005

	school notes/homework	what's on this week
monday **20**	Frank Lampard, 27 today	
tuesday **21**	Longest Day	
wednesday **22**	Maradona knocks England out of the World Cup with his infamous 'hand of God' goal, 1986	
thursday **23**	Zinedine Zidane, 33 today Patrick Vieira, 29 today	
friday **24**		
saturday **25**		
sunday **26**	Beckham scores his first goal for England (vs Columbia in the World Cup), 1998	

FACTS OF THE WEEK

STONE ME!

Some fish look like stones. Stone fish rest on the seabed, looking just like the rocks that surround them. If they are spotted, the poisonous spines on their backs can stun an attacker in seconds.

PIED PIPER

The legend of the Pied Piper tells of how, in 1284, a mysterious piper rid the town of Hamelin in Germany of its plague of rats. When the piper played his pipe, all the rats followed him to their deaths.

ESCAPOLOGIST

The Hungarian-born American Harry Houdini (1874-1926) was one of the world's greatest showmen, and the most famous 'escapologist', or escape artist. He was able to escape from chains and handcuffs while locked in a safe or immersed in a tank of water.

MIND PUZZLE

How many sporting events make up a decathlon

JOKE OF THE WEEK

"Which team plays in its underwear?"
"Vest Brom!"

June/July 2005

	school notes/homework	what's on this week
monday **27**	Raul (Gonzalez Blanco), 28 today	
tuesday **28**	Fabian Barthez, 34 today	
wednesday **29**		
thursday **30**	Darius Vassell, 25 today	
friday **1**	Patrick Kluivert, 29 today Ruud van Nistelrooy, 29 today	
saturday **2**		
sunday **3**		

FACTS OF THE WEEK

KEEP WELL AWAY!

The Australian redback spider is one of the most deadly of a group called widow spiders. These spiders get their name because, once they have mated, the female may well eat the male!

CROP CIRCLES

Since the 1980s, mysterious patterns have appeared in fields of wheat in Europe and North America. Known as 'crop circles' - though they may be any shape. No one knows for certain who or what has made them - disease, jokers or even aliens!

WELL-BRED

You may be happy with your street tabby but in the cat-show world pedigrees count for everything. The forward-folded ears of this Scottish fold cat are considered a deformity in Europe, but the cat is popular in the United States.

QUICK QUIZ

1. Who was Sven Goran Eriksson's first captain for England?
2. Bastia play in which country's league?
3. Which club play home games at Bramall Lane?
4. How many caps did Glenn Hoddle win for England?
5. Who plays their home games at Tannadice Park?
6. What was the name of the dog that found the World Cup in 1966?

1. David Beckham 2. France 3. Sheffield United 4. 53 5. Dundee United 6. Pickles

NUMBER PUZZLE

Which number should replace the question mark?

1 3 5 7
11 13 17 19 ?
29 31 37 39 41

23 – They are all prime numbers

☆ July 2005

	school notes/homework	what's on this week
monday **4**	England lose 1990 World Cup semi-final on penalties to West Germany	
tuesday **5**	Hernan Crespo, 30 today	
wednesday **6**		
thursday **7**		
friday **8**	Robbie Keane, 25 today	
saturday **9**		
sunday **10**		

FACTS OF THE WEEK

DIVING FOR THEIR DINNER

Leatherbacks dive up to 120 metres for dinner. These turtles hold the record for being the biggest sea turtles and for making the deepest dives. Leatherbacks feed mostly on jellyfish but their diet also includes molluscs and other shellfish.

THE SPEEDY SPACE BALL

The Earth is a huge ball of rock moving through space at nearly 3000 metres per second. It weights 600 million, million, million tonnes. Up to two-thirds of the Earth's rocky surface is covered by water – this makes the seas and oceans. Rock that is not covered by water makes the land.

FIERY PHOENIX

The phoenix was a magical bird that lived for 500 years without eating or drinking. It lived in the deserts of the Middle East. When the time came for it to die, it set fire to itself. But it was reborn from its own ashes after three days, ready to live again.

JOKE OF THE WEEK

"Which team tastes best on toast?"
"West Jam!"

WORD SEARCH

Can you find the names of five sports hidden below?

S	Q	N	I	F	S	D	T
Q	K	P	O	L	O	L	E
U	W	D	W	O	P	S	N
A	H	O	C	K	E	Y	N
S	C	W	I	P	K	D	I
H	F	O	J	B	I	L	S
K	R	U	G	B	Y	X	T
M	U	M	F	O	R	A	B

July 2005

	school notes/homework	what's on this week
monday **11**		
tuesday **12**	Christian Vieri, 32 today	
wednesday **13**	Craig Bellamy, 26 today	
thursday **14**		
friday **15**		
saturday **16**		
sunday **17**		

FACTS OF THE WEEK

THE RUIN OF ARTHUR

Lancelot was the favourite knight of King Arthur. Tales of Arthur and his Knights of the Round Table were very popular in the 1200s. Lancelot fell in love with Arthur's wife Guinevere. The struggle between the two men eventually destroyed Arthur's court.

PUNCH AND JUDY

This traditional English form of puppet show, based on the old Italian farces of the "Commedia dell'Arte" dated back to the 1700's. The stories revolve around the cruel and boastful Mr Punch and his loud-mouthed wife Judy.

SPEEDY SATELLITE

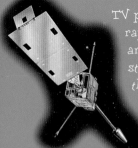

TV pictures and sound can be sent rapidly around the world. They are transmitted to satellites in stationary orbit in space, and then redirected to another part of the world. This means that live news can be broadcast immediately.

JOKE OF THE WEEK
"Why is Cinderella rubbish at football?"
"She keeps running away from the ball!"

QUICK QUIZ

1. In what year did Sven Goran Eriksson take charge of the England team?

2. With which club was Bobby Moore when he was made captain of England?

3. What shirt number did Eric Cantona wear when playing for Man Utd?

4. Which club plays its home games at White Hart Lane?

5. In what season was the Premiership league launched?

6. What colour do Italy play in for their home games?

1. 2001 2. West Ham 3. No. 7 4. Tottenham Hotspur 5. 1992-93 6. Blue

ODD ONE OUT

Which of these names is the ODD ONE OUT and why?

ALEX, TIM, SAM, LOU

Tim – All the others are for both boys and girls

July 2005

	school notes/homework	what's on this week
monday **18**		
tuesday **19**		
wednesday **20**		
thursday **21**		
friday **22**		
saturday **23**		
sunday **24**		

FACTS OF THE WEEK

GOING FISHING

Few creatures can survive in the dark, icy-cold ocean depths. Food is so hard to come by, the deep-sea anglerfish does not waste energy chasing prey – it has developed a clever fishing trick. A stringy 'fishing rod' with a glowing tip attracts smaller fish to the anglerfish's big mouth.

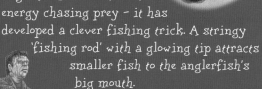

FRANKENSTEIN'S MONSTER

Created by writer Mary Shelley in 1818, Frankenstein's monster was made from dead corpses joined together. At first friendly, it turned violent and began to kill people. Frankenstein blamed himself for meddling with nature.

COLOUR WHEEL

The three primary colours are red, yellow, and blue. These can be mixed together to form orange, green and purple. On a colour wheel, one primary colour will appear opposite the mixture of the two other primary colours. These opposites are called complementary colours.

MIND PUZZLE

How many minutes are there in five hours?

JOKE OF THE WEEK

"What's a snake's favourite footie team?"
"Slitherpool!"

July 2005

	school notes/homework	what's on this week
monday **25**	Kevin Phillips, 32 today	
tuesday **26**		
wednesday **27**		
thursday **28**	Michael Carrick, 24 today	
friday **29**		
saturday **30**	Uruguay win the first World Cup, 1930 England win the World Cup, 1966	
sunday **31**		

FACTS OF THE WEEK

DON'T FORGET THE SUNSCREEN!

Sunfish like sunbathing! Ocean sunfish are very large, broad fish that can weigh as much as 1 tonne. They are named after their habit of sunbathing on the surface of the open ocean.

BUNDLE OF FUN

Baby dinosaurs grew up to five times faster than human babies! A baby sauropod dinosaur like Diplodocus was already 1 metre long and 30 kilograms in weight when it came out of its egg!

BLOODTHIRSTY VAMPIRES

There are many stories of vampires – dead bodies that have returned to life. By day they look like ordinary people, but at night they grow wings like bats and their teeth change into fangs. The most famous vampire was Count Dracula.

JOKE OF THE WEEK

"What kind of money do goalies make?"
"Net profits!"

QUICK QUIZ

1. What surname links England players Ashley, Andy and Joe?

2. In which year was Sir Alex Fergusson born: 1941, 1951 or 1961?

3. With which club did Nicky Butt begin his career?

4. In which city was David Beckham born: London, Liverpool or Manchester?

5. WET MASH is an anagram of which football club?

6. Which player moved from Leeds to Man United in the summer of 2002?

1. Cole 2. 1941 3. Man United 4. London 5. West Ham 6. Rio Ferdinand

WORD SCRAMBLE

Unscramble the letters to find three famous English landmarks

NOTESGEHEN, GIB NEB, SELONNS NUMLOC

STONEHENGE, BIG BEN, NELSON'S COLUMN

Football
Facts and figures

Everyone loves making lists and we're no different. Here are some from the world of football you might find interesting.

Top 5 Highest transfer fees

1	Zinedine Zidane £48.0 million	when he moved from Juventus to Real Madrid in the summer of 2001
2	Luis Figo £37.5 million	when he moved from Barcelona to Real Madrid in the summer of 2000
3	Hernan Crespo £35.4 million	when he moved from Parma to Lazio in the summer of 2000
4	Gianluigi Buffon £32.6 million	when he moved from Parma to Juventus in the summer of 2001
5	Christian Vieri £31.0 million	when he moved from Lazio to Inter Milan in the summer of 1999

Premiership winners

Since the Premiership began in 1992. Before that the top of the English league was Division One.

1992/93	Manchester United
1993/94	Manchester United
1994/95	Blackburn Rovers
1995/96	Manchester United
1996/97	Manchester United
1997/98	Arsenal
1998/99	Manchester United
1999/00	Manchester United
2000/01	Manchester United
2001/02	Arsenal
2002/03	Manchester United

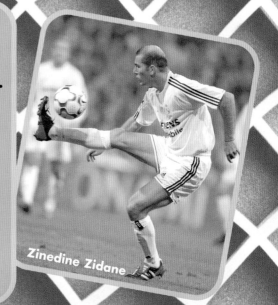

Zinedine Zidane

Most FA Cup wins

The FA Cup is the oldest football competition in the world! It's loved by fans in England as small teams get the chance to compete against the bigger, richer clubs and show them up if they knock out the giants!

	Club	Wins	Last win	Runners-up	Last losing final
1	Manchester United	10	1999	5	1995
2	Arsenal	9	2003	7	2001
3	Tottenham Hotspur	8	1991	1	1987
4	Aston Villa	7	1957	3	2000
5	Newcastle United	6	1955	7	1999
6	Liverpool	6	2001	6	1996
7	Blackburn Rovers	6	1928	2	1960
8	Everton	5	1995	7	1989
9	West Bromwich Albion	5	1968	5	1935
10	Wanderers FC	5	1878	0	–

Top 10 UEFA Champions League winners

Most wins and runners-up

	Wins	Runners-up
Real Madrid	9	3
AC Milan	6	3
FC Bayern	4	3
Ajax Amsterdam	4	2
Liverpool	4	1
Juventus	2	5
Benfica	2	5
Inter Milan	2	2
Manchester Utd	2	0
Nottingham Forest	2	0

Top 5 Europe's biggest stadiums

Stadiums used by football clubs, according to the number of fans each can hold.

1 Nou Camp	Barcelona	98,600
2 San Siro	Inter and AC Milan	85,840
3 Olimpiysky Stadion	Dynamo Kiev	83,160
4 Westfalenstadion	Borussia Dortmund	83,000
5 Stadio Olimpico	Lazio and Roma	82,920

The seven British stadiums in the Top 50

16 Millennium Stadium	Cardiff*	72,500
21 Old Trafford	Manchester United	68,170
25 Celtic Park	Glasgow Celtic	60,500
36 St James' Park	Newcastle United	52,210
39 Hampden Park	Queen's Park**	52,000
44 Ibrox Park	Glasgow Rangers	50,420
50 City of Manchester Stadium	Man City	48,000

* used by Welsh national side and for English Cup finals
** also used by Scottish national side as home ground

The World

TOP 10

Our planet is a pretty fascinating place, and if you don't believe us take a look at some of these stunning stats...

TOP 10 COUNTRIES BY POPULATION

1. CHINA 1.28 BILLION
2. INDIA 1.04BN
3. USA 280 MILLION
4. INDONESIA 231M
5. BRAZIL 176M
6. PAKISTAN 147M
7. RUSSIA 144M
8. BANGLADESH 133M
9. JAPAN 129M
10. NIGERIA 129M

TOP 10 MOST SPOKEN LANGUAGES

1. CHINESE MANDARIN 1.075BN
2. ENGLISH 514M
3. HINDUSTANI 496M
4. SPANISH 425M
5. RUSSIAN 275M
6. ARABIC 256M
7. BENGALI 215M
8. PORTUGUESE 194M
9. MALAY-INDONESIAN 176M
10. FRENCH 129M

TOP 10 COUNTRIES BY NUMBER OF TELEVISIONS

1. **CHINA 400M**
2. **USA 219M**
3. **JAPAN 86.5M**
4. **INDIA 63M**
5. **RUSSIA 60M**
6. **GERMANY 51M**
7. **BRAZIL 36.5M**
8. **FRANCE 34M**
9. **UK 30M**
10. **UKRAINE 18M**

TOP 10 TALLEST BUILDINGS

1. **TAIPEI 101 TOWER, TAIPEI, 508M**
2. **SHANGHAI WORLD FINANCIAL CENTRE, CHINA, 460M**
3. **PETRONAS TOWERS, KUALA LUMPUR, 452M**
4. **SEARS TOWER, CHICAGO, 442M**
5. **JIN MAO BUILDING, SHANGHAI, 421M**
6. **TWO INTERNATIONAL FINANCE CENTER, HONG KONG, 412M**
7. **SKY CENTRAL/CITI PLAZA, GUANGZHOU, 391M**
8. **SHUN HING SQUARE, SHENZHEN, 384M**
9. **EMPIRE STATE BUILDING, NYC, 381M**
10. **CENTRAL PLAZA, HONG KONG, 374M**

PHONE A FRIEND

NAME _____ NAME _____
PHONE _____ PHONE _____
ADDRESS _____ ADDRESS _____
_____ _____
_____ _____
E-MAIL _____ E-MAIL _____

NAME _____ NAME _____
PHONE _____ PHONE _____
ADDRESS _____ ADDRESS _____
_____ _____
_____ _____
E-MAIL _____ E-MAIL _____

NAME _____ NAME _____
PHONE _____ PHONE _____
ADDRESS _____ ADDRESS _____
_____ _____
_____ _____
E-MAIL _____ E-MAIL _____

NAME _____ NAME _____
PHONE _____ PHONE _____
ADDRESS _____ ADDRESS _____
_____ _____
_____ _____
E-MAIL _____ E-MAIL _____

NAME _____ NAME _____
PHONE _____ PHONE _____
ADDRESS _____ ADDRESS _____
_____ _____
_____ _____
E-MAIL _____ E-MAIL _____

NAME

PHONE

ADDRESS

E-MAIL

NAME

PHONE

ADDRESS

E-MAIL

NAME

PHONE

ADDRESS

E-MAIL

NAME

PHONE

ADDRESS

E-MAIL

NAME

PHONE

ADDRESS

E-MAIL

NAME

PHONE

ADDRESS

E-MAIL

NAME

PHONE

ADDRESS

E-MAIL

NAME

PHONE

ADDRESS

E-MAIL

NAME

PHONE

ADDRESS

E-MAIL

NAME

PHONE

ADDRESS

E-MAIL

PHONE A FRIEND

NAME _____

PHONE _____

ADDRESS _____

_____

_____

E-MAIL _____

NAME _____

PHONE _____

ADDRESS _____

_____

_____

E-MAIL _____

NAME _____

PHONE _____

ADDRESS _____

_____

_____

E-MAIL _____

NAME _____

PHONE _____

ADDRESS _____

_____

_____

E-MAIL _____

NAME _____

PHONE _____

ADDRESS _____

_____

_____

E-MAIL _____

NAME _____

PHONE _____

ADDRESS _____

_____

_____

E-MAIL _____

NAME _____

PHONE _____

ADDRESS _____

_____

_____

E-MAIL _____

NAME _____

PHONE _____

ADDRESS _____

_____

_____

E-MAIL _____

NAME _____

PHONE _____

ADDRESS _____

_____

_____

E-MAIL _____

NAME _____

PHONE _____

ADDRESS _____

_____

_____

E-MAIL _____

NAME		NAME	
PHONE		PHONE	
ADDRESS		ADDRESS	
E-MAIL		E-MAIL	

NAME		NAME	
PHONE		PHONE	
ADDRESS		ADDRESS	
E-MAIL		E-MAIL	

NAME		NAME	
PHONE		PHONE	
ADDRESS		ADDRESS	
E-MAIL		E-MAIL	

NAME		NAME	
PHONE		PHONE	
ADDRESS		ADDRESS	
E-MAIL		E-MAIL	

NAME		NAME	
PHONE		PHONE	
ADDRESS		ADDRESS	
E-MAIL		E-MAIL	

First published by Bardfield Press in 2004

Bardfield Press is an imprint of
Miles Kelly Publishing Ltd
Bardfield Centre, Great Bardfield, Essex CM7 4SL

2 4 6 8 10 9 7 5 3 1

Project Manager
Lisa Clayden

Designers
Michelle Cannatella, Andy Knight, Debbie Meekcoms

Cover Designer
Louisa Leitao

Editorial Director
Belinda Gallagher

Picture Researcher
Liberty Newton, Jenni Hunt

Production Manager
Estela Boulton

British Library Cataloguing-in-Publication Data
A catalogue record for this book is available from the British Library

ISBN 1-84236-449-9

Printed in Hong Kong

The publishers wish to thank the following artists who have contributed to this book:
Andy Beckett (Linden Artists), Dave Burrows, Jim Channell, Kuo Kang Chen, Mark Davies,
Peter Dennis, Richard Draper, Wayne Ford, Terry Gabbey, Luigi Galante, Alan Hancocks,
Sally Holmes, Richard Hook (Linden Artists), Rob Jakeway, John James (Temple Rogers), Steve Kirk,
Mick Loates (Linden Artists) Andy Lloyd Jones, Kevin Maddison, Alan Male, Janos Marffy,
Massimiliano Maugeri (Galante Studios), Angus McBride, Doreen McGuinness, Andrea Morandi,
Tracey Morgan, Steve Roberts Martin Sanders, Peter Sarson, Rob Sheffield, Ted Smart, Nick Spender
Roger Stewart, Gwen Touret, Rudi Vizi, Christian Webb Steve Weston, Mike White (Temple Rogers)

The publishers wish to thank the following sources for the photographs used in this book:

Cover photograph:
Adrian Dennis/AFP/GETTY IMAGES

Inside photographs:
AFP/GETTY IMAGES; Adrian Dennis/AFP/GETTY IMAGES
Gerry Penny/AFP/GETTY IMAGES; Nicola Casamassima/AFP/GETTY IMAGES
Javier Soriano/AFP/GETTY IMAGES Buena Vista/Walt Disney/Pictorial Press; Pictorial Press

All other pictures from Corel, Digital STOCK, Dover Publications, Hemera, ILN
The publishers would like to thank Great Bardfield Primary School for their advice.

Third party website addresses are provided by Miles Kelly Publishing in good faith and for information only
and were suitable and accurate at the time of going to press.
Miles Kelly Publishing disclaims any responsiblity for the material contained therein.

e-mail: info@mileskelly.net

www.mileskelly.net